SEE & EXPLORE
LIBRARY

ANIMALS
and WHERE THEY LIVE

Written by
John Feltwell, Ph.D.

DORLING KINDERSLEY, INC.
NEW YORK

A DORLING KINDERSLEY BOOK

Editor Angela Wilkes
U.S. editor B. Alison Weir
Art editor Roger Priddy

Editorial director Jackie Douglas
Art director Roger Bristow

Illustrated by
John Rignall, Phil Weare, Ian Jackson,
Bob Bampton, Alan Male, Helen Senior,
Dee Morgan and Giuliano Forani

10 9 8 7 6

Dorling Kindersley, Inc., 95 Madison Avenue
New York, New York 10016

Library of Congress Cataloging-in-Publication Data
Feltwell, John
Animals; and where they live / by John Feltwell - 2nd American ed.
p. cm. - (See & Explore library) Includes index.
Summary: Captioned illustrations present information about a variety
of animals, birds, fish, and insects, describing what they eat, where
they live, and how they raise their young.
ISBN 1-879431-99-8 (trade)
ISBN 1-56458-000-8 (lib. bdg.)
1. Animals - Juvenile literature. 2. Habitat (Ecology) - Juvenile
literature. [1. Animals.] I. Series
[QL49.F416 1992]   91-58202
591-dc20   CIP AC

Phototypeset by SX Composing, Essex
Reproduced in Singapore by Colourscan
Printed in Spain by Artes Graficas; Toledo S.A.
D.L.TO:918-1995

CONTENTS

SPECIAL ANIMALS, SPECIAL PLACES

Just as we have our own special place to live, so animals have theirs. Animals live everywhere on Earth – on the land and in the sea, in every kind of terrain and in different types of climate. Most animals have lived in the same part of the world for thousands of years. As a result, they have developed a way of life that helps them fit into a particular place and climate. Each animal's own special living place is called its *habitat*.

Because habitats are so different from each other, only certain animals can live in each one. Some fish, for example, need to live in fresh water. If they were put into the sea they would die. But a saltwater fish, such as a mackerel, could not survive if it was put into fresh water. For the same reason, penguins would die if moved to the desert, and scorpions would perish on the polar ice cap. It is true that you can go to a European or American safari park and see lions and other animals living quite happily, far from their original home on the African savannah. But many animals can only be kept alive outside their natural habitat if they are in zoos or aquariums. And while it is interesting to watch animals in captivity, to find out about how they really live we need to look at them in their natural surroundings.

Where animals live

By watching animals in their own habitats we can see how they find food, make their homes, and bring up their young. We can also observe them as part of a whole community of different animals. Throughout the world, communities of animals live in widely differing habitats, ranging from burning deserts to the frozen wastes of the polar regions. By looking at each of the major environments around the world, we can find out more about how animals live.

A zoo in grand surroundings

Seeing different types of animals grouped together in the grand setting of a stately home makes you realize how very different our habitats are from those of animals. Can you imagine how you and your friends would look sitting in a rabbit warren or perched on top of a tree! In fact all the animals in the picture can survive away from their natural habitats, provided they have food, warmth, and shelter.

4

Pigeon

Llama

Gibbon

Kangaroo

Kestrel

Goat

Cheetah

Lion

Parrot

Raccoon

Guinea pig

Otter

Dog

Red fox

Lizard

Weasel

Duck

Skunk

Rabbit

Terrapin

5

PICTURE MAP

The remarkable ability of animals to adapt to their surroundings has enabled them to colonize the wide variety of habitats that exist on Earth. Similar types of habitat are found in different places around the world and similar types of animals often live in them. The same kinds of animals live in the forests and tundra of North America and the USSR. Likewise, the same types of animals graze on

the grasslands of South America, Africa, and Australia. The biggest habitat on Earth is the sea, which provides a home for some of the largest as well as the smallest creatures in the world. Wherever animals live, they have to compete for food and shelter. Nature maintains a fine balance so that different types of animals are able to live together in the same habitat.

Coniferous forest
A band of dense, evergreen forest stretches right across the top of Europe, Asia, and North America. Here animals have to be able to cope with long, hard winters. *See pages 20-21 for more on forests.*

Marshlands
Half land and half water, marshes are usually found near estuaries, lakes, and rivers. They provide a home for a wide variety of wildlife, particularly birds. *See pages 34-35 for more on marshlands.*

Islands
All islands are different and many of them provide a home for strange and totally unique plants and animals that are not found anywhere else in the world. *See pages 24-25 to find out about animals that live on islands.*

Oceans
The oceans cover about three-quarters of the Earth's surface. There are warm seas near the Equator and frozen seas near the Poles. *See pages 56-57 for more on oceans.*

Jungles
It rains nearly every day in the hot jungles, or rain forests, that grow near the Equator. More types of plants and animals live there than anywhere else. *See pages 44-47 for more on jungles.*

Homes around the world
On this picture map you can see where the different types of habitats are all around the world. You can also see some of the animals that live in each area.

Arctic Ocean

North America

Rocky Mountains

Atlantic Ocean

Amazon jungle

South America

Antarctica

Polar regions
Amazingly, some animals and plants manage to thrive in the frozen wastes and seas of the Arctic and Antarctica. *See pages 8-11 for more on life in the polar regions.*

Shrublands
Sun-parched countryside, dotted with tough shrubs and aromatic herbs, is common around the Mediterranean. *See pages 26-29 for more on shrublands.*

Deciduous forest
These are found mostly in Europe and North America where the climate is mild and damp. *See pages 22-23 to find out more about life in a single tree of the deciduous forest.*

Mountains
A wide range of habitats, ranging from lush forest on the lower slopes to bleak tundra higher up, can be found on a mountain. *See pages 14-17 to find out more about mountains.*

USSR

Europe

Mediterranean

Africa

Himalayas

Asia

Savannah

Pacific Ocean

Equator

Australia

Deserts
Deserts are the driest places on Earth. It rarely rains, but many plants and animals have adapted to life in these harsh conditions. *See pages 50-53 for more on deserts.*

Grasslands
The great grasslands of the world stretch for thousands of miles. These dry, grassy plains provide food for huge herds of grazing animals. *See pages 38-41 for more on grasslands.*

Coral reef
A coral reef is an exotic underwater kingdom, teeming with animals and plants. Corals are found in shallow sunlit, tropical waters. *See pages 58-59 for more on coral reefs.*

A WORLD OF ICE

The polar regions are a hostile world of ice and snow. The winters can last for up to nine months, with subzero temperatures, raging blizzards, and total darkness for much of the time. During the brief summer months there is daylight for nearly 24 hours a day. The temperature rises above freezing and some of the ice melts. It seems as if nothing could live in these frozen wastes, yet, astonishingly, there are many plants and animals that survive and even flourish there.

The Arctic Ocean stretches across the North Pole. It is covered in ice for most of the year, yet fish, seals, and whales live there in vast numbers, feeding on the rich supply of tiny plants and animals, called plankton, that live in it. The ocean is surrounded by frozen land called tundra. Tough bushes and plants grow on the tundra and in the spring and summer it comes alive with insects, birds, and small mammals, such as lemmings and hares.

Conditions are even harder on Antarctica, the frozen continent around the South Pole. Little survives on Antarctica itself, but the seas around it are swarming with life. Here and on the next two pages we take a closer look at life in a world of ice.

Polar bear
The polar bear is an excellent swimmer and its thick fur keeps it warm in the water as well as on land. It spends most of its time roaming the sea ice in search of seals to eat.

Walruses
Walruses usually live in herds. They move northward with the ice pack as it melts in spring and swim south ahead of the freezing sea in autumn, feeding on shellfish from the seabed.

Arctic tern
Like many other birds, the Arctic tern is a summer visitor to the Arctic and nests along the coasts. In the autumn it migrates all the way to Antarctica, where summer is coming.

Arctic tern

Beluga

Polar bear

Oldsquaw ducks

Blackfish

Cod

The great thaw
When spring arrives in the Arctic, the ice begins to thaw. Flowers come into bloom on the tundra and there is a sudden burst of activity among the animals. As food supplies become more plentiful, birds start nesting on the high cliffs overlooking the ice and animals rear their young.

Narwhal
The male narwhal whale has a long, twisted tusk that looks similar to a unicorn's horn. No one knows what it is for, but males have been seen sparring with them.

Cod and blackfish
In spring, huge shoals of cod and blackfish swim into the Arctic Ocean to feed on the plankton and to spawn. They provide invaluable food for the seals and seabirds.

Skuas and jaegers
Both of these birds are predators. Skuas like to steal other birds' food and will eat any dead birds or animals (carrion) they find. Jaegers are long-tailed skuas that eat lemmings and fish.

Puffins and murres
Huge colonies of puffins and murres nest on steep cliffs above the ice. Puffins lay their eggs in shallow burrows in soft cliff-top soil. Murres nest on ledges. Their eggs are pear-shaped, so they do not roll.

Puffins

Jaeger

Skua

Murres

Hooded seals

Harp seals

Bearded seal

Ribbon seal

Hooded seals
Hooded seals spend most of their lives in the sea, but come onto the ice to mate and breed. The males have large noses which inflate like balloons when they are courting.

Ivory gulls
Ivory gulls are the only seabirds that are totally white in color. This helps to protect them from predators, because they are difficult to see against the snowy landscape.

Bear families
Female polar bears give birth to their cubs in the safety of a snow den, deep inside a snow bank. The mother goes without food for up to six months while she looks after her cubs.

Ringed seals
These seals·also live mainly in the sea, but they can only stay underwater for 20 minutes at a time. They chew breathing holes in the ice, so that they can come up for air.

9

SURVIVING THE COLD

The animals and birds that live near the North and South Poles have evolved in unique ways to cope with life in icy conditions. Mammals such as polar bears and foxes have a thick outer coat of long, shaggy hair and a soft, fleecy layer of fur closer to their skin, so they are doubly protected against the cold. Whales, polar bears, and seals have thick layers of oil-rich fat under their skin, and birds that spend the winter in the polar regions have thick plumage and fluff out their feathers to keep warm. Some insects hibernate in the winter and have a special chemical in their blood which acts like anti-freeze and stops their blood from freezing.

The animals that live on land or the ice have to be able to walk across the snow easily. Polar bears have big, wide feet that act like snowshoes and birds such as ptarmigan and grouse have feathers on the soles of their feet.

As well as coping with the cold, animals have to time very carefully when they mate and give birth. Most animals breed during the brief summer months when it is warmer and food is plentiful.

Breeding on the ice
Penguins are the only birds that are able to breed in the freezing conditions on Antarctica. Most of them breed in the spring in huge rookeries inland from the sea, but the emperor penguins, shown here, breed on the ice-covered sea in the depths of winter.

The largest penguins
The emperor penguins are the largest of all penguins. They can be 4 ft (1.2 m) tall. Like all penguins, they are admirably adapted to life in the water. Their short wings act as paddles, their webbed feet help them to steer, and their bodies are streamlined.

Speedy swimmers
Penguins cannot fly and look clumsy on land. They waddle along or slither on their bellies. They are more at home underwater, where they can swim at up to 25 mph (40 kph). To get back on to the ice, they shoot out of the water at speed and land upright on their feet.

Winter eggs
Emperors do not breed at the same time as other penguins, but in the middle of winter when the temperature is well below freezing. The male and female penguins have very different roles. The female lays a single egg, and immediately dives into the sea and swims away.

Incubating the egg

The male then balances the egg on his feet and covers it with part of his body, a special sort of pouch, to keep it warm. For 64 days, in pitch darkness and through blizzards the penguin stands there, incubating his egg.

The chick hatches

During that time, the penguin does not eat and gets much thinner. When the ice breaks up in the spring, the female returns, just as the chick hatches. The male is free to go and find food, then both parents care for the chick.

Changing color

Many of the animals and birds that live in the Arctic change the color of their feathers or fur with the changing seasons, so that they are well camouflaged all year long. They do this by molting. Predators, such as Arctic foxes, have coats that change from brown in the summer to white in the winter. So do the creatures they prey on, such as hares and ptarmigan. If they all stayed brown in winter, they would easily be seen against the white snow.

Arctic fox

Arctic hare

Ptarmigan

Winter underground

In the Arctic winter, while many animals sleep, life goes on beneath the snow. Lemmings live in a maze of burrows and runs below the surface of the tundra, and the layers of snow act like a quilt, helping to keep them warm. The lemmings feed on roots and underground shoots and continue breeding all winter. They do not emerge from the burrows until the snow melts in late spring and food is more plentiful above the ground.

| Surface run | Layer of snow | Vegetation | Nest |

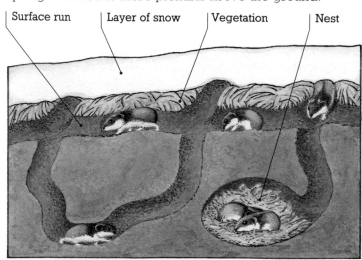

THE LARGEST ANIMALS

The largest animals ever to roam the Earth were the dinosaurs, which died out 65 million years ago. The largest of them may have been as long as 74 ft (22.5 m) and weighed up to 90 tons.

Nowadays the African elephant is the largest animal living on land, but both in size and weight it is dwarfed by the largest animal of all: the blue whale. This marine giant is both longer and heavier than the biggest dinosaur that ever lived. For the blue whale it is actually an advantage to be big. Its great size helps it to keep warm in cold water. How large an animal is depends on where it lives and what it eats. The elephant is probably big partly because it needs a big stomach to digest all the tough plants it eats. Its size also helps to protect it, as few predators would dare to attack it.

Large animals used to have few enemies, but now they are at the mercy of the most dangerous predators of all, humans, and many of them are being hunted to the point of extinction.

The giants of the animal world
Here some of the biggest animals are grouped together to show how big they are in relation to one another. As you can see, those that live on land are dwarfed by those that live in the sea.

The biggest animal
The blue whale is the biggest mammal in the world. It is over 100 ft (30 m) long and can weigh 190 tons. Incredibly, the blue whale has no teeth and lives entirely on a diet of tiny shrimplike creatures called krill.

The largest fish
The rare plankton-eating whale shark is about 55 ft (16.8 m) long and weighs 37 tons. This makes it the biggest fish in the world.

Tallest living mammal
The average height of the Masai giraffe of East Africa is 17 ft 4½ in (5.3 m), making it taller than any other animal. Its long neck enables it to feed from the tops of acacia trees and thorny bushes on the plains where it lives.

The largest on land
The African elephant stands about 10 ft 6 in (3.2 m) tall at the shoulder and weighs over 5 tons. It once roamed over most of Africa but its numbers have now declined and it is confined mainly to wildlife parks and game preserves.

The biggest bird
At 8 ft (2.4 m) tall, the African ostrich is the largest bird in the world. It is also the fastest running bird, as it can run at speeds of up to 45 miles (72 km) an hour, but it cannot fly. Other giant flightless birds are the emu, the rhea, and the cassowary.

Elephant

Man

Ostrich

Giraffe

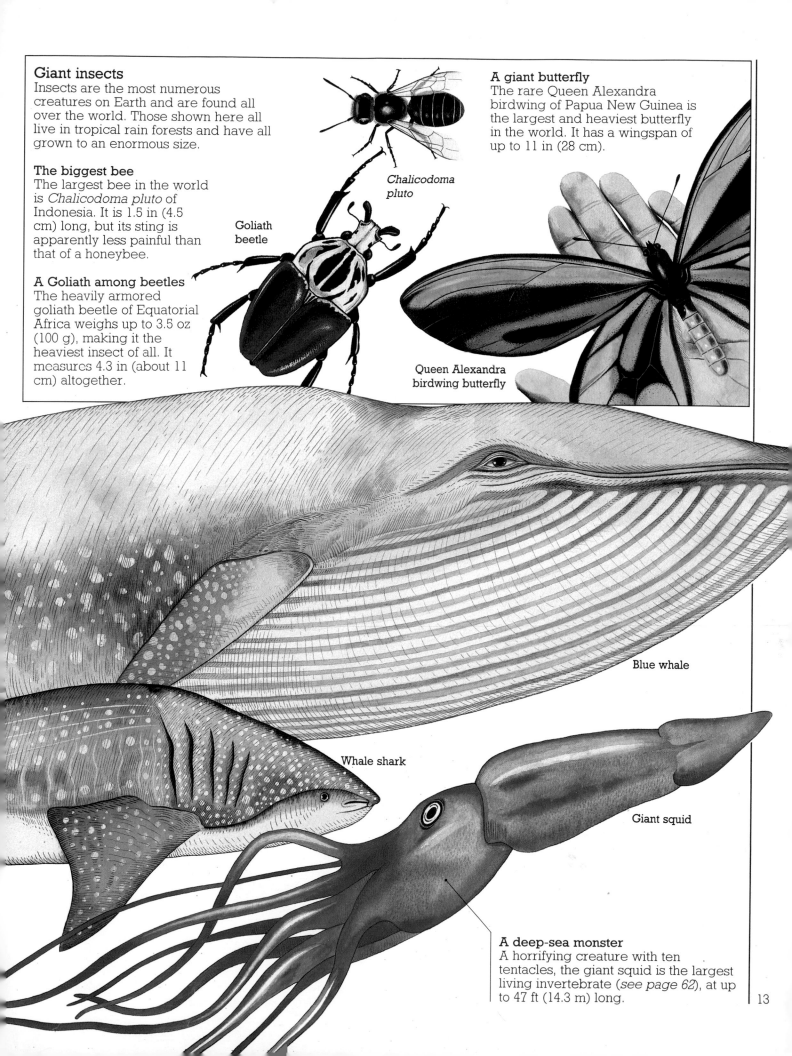

Giant insects

Insects are the most numerous creatures on Earth and are found all over the world. Those shown here all live in tropical rain forests and have all grown to an enormous size.

The biggest bee

The largest bee in the world is *Chalicodoma pluto* of Indonesia. It is 1.5 in (4.5 cm) long, but its sting is apparently less painful than that of a honeybee.

A Goliath among beetles

The heavily armored goliath beetle of Equatorial Africa weighs up to 3.5 oz (100 g), making it the heaviest insect of all. It measures 4.3 in (about 11 cm) altogether.

A giant butterfly

The rare Queen Alexandra birdwing of Papua New Guinea is the largest and heaviest butterfly in the world. It has a wingspan of up to 11 in (28 cm).

Chalicodoma pluto

Goliath beetle

Queen Alexandra birdwing butterfly

Blue whale

Whale shark

Giant squid

A deep-sea monster

A horrifying creature with ten tentacles, the giant squid is the largest living invertebrate (*see page 62*), at up to 47 ft (14.3 m) long.

13

LIFE IN THE MOUNTAINS

On every mountain, within the short distance from its base to its peak, there is a wide variety of different habitats, ranging from dense forest to bare rocky ground. This is because weather conditions change all the way up a mountain. The lower slopes often have a lot of mist or rain, but as you climb higher, the air becomes cooler and drier. This affects the type of trees and plants that grow at each level, and from a distance quite distinct bands of vegetation can be seen merging into one another all the way up the mountain.

As you climb a mountain, you move first through tropical or deciduous forest, depending on which part of the world you are in, then into coniferous forest. Next you come to the "tree line," where the trees end. No trees can grow above this height, which varies depending on the weather conditions and where the mountain is. Above the tree line are grassy meadows, then rocky ground, and finally, on high mountains, a snow-covered peak. Different animals live in each band of vegetation. You can find out more about them on the next page.

Life at different levels

Here you can see how the plant and animal life changes at different levels on an imaginary mountain in the Himalayas. The highest mountains in the world, the Himalaya range, are 1,500 miles (2,400 km) long and 20,000 ft (6,000 m) high on average.

Lammergeier

Wild yak

Markhor goat

Apollo butterfly

Lesser panda

Snowcock

Black bear

Tiger

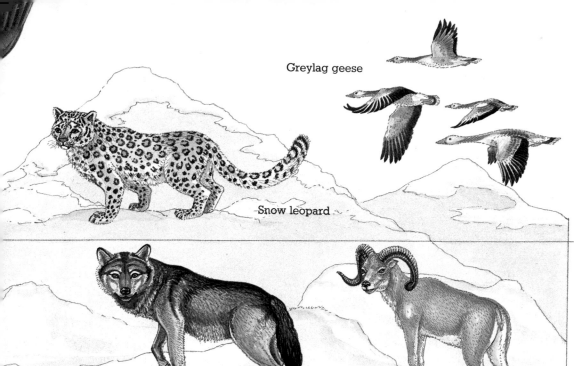

Greylag geese

Snow leopard

Snow and rocks
It is very cold at the top of a high mountain and no plants can grow there. The Himalayas are so high that their peaks are covered in snow and ice all year round. The snow leopard occasionally ventures up high, and sharp-eyed birds of prey soar above the slopes.

Wolf

Argali

Alpine tundra
The tundra zone is similar in appearance to the Arctic tundra (see page 10). The rocky ground is dotted with icy pools in winter and sprinkled with flowers in spring. Grazing animals like the wild yak and the argali, the world's largest mountain sheep, feed there in the summer.

Himalayan monal

Wild ass

Alpine meadow
Above the tree line are lush grassy meadows. It is still very cold here and plants have to be tough to survive the harsh conditions. They have long roots and grow close to the ground. Wild asses and mountain goats, such as the markhor, graze on the meadows in the summer.

Bhutan glory

Tahr

Pikas

Coniferous forest
Conifers, such as the pine and fir, flourish in the cold, dry mountain air. Their resin protects them from hungry insects, but their cones provide seeds for birds to eat. The lesser panda, an agile tree climber, lives in these forests, as does the tahr, a type of mountain goat.

Serows (goat antelopes)

Langur

Deciduous forests
The deciduous forests of the foothills provide food and shelter for a wide variety of animals. Langur monkeys eat the fruit and leaves of the trees and move higher up the mountain during the summer. Bears and tigers roam the forested slopes at the base of the mountain.

LIFE AT THE TOP

The higher you go up a mountain, the colder the air becomes, dropping by 3.6°F (2°C) every 1,000 ft (300 m) you climb. It also becomes thinner and contains less oxygen. Mountain animals have thick, warm fur and strong lungs to help them cope with the cold, wind, snow, and the thin air. They are also surefooted so that they don't lose their grip on steep, rocky slopes. Many of them move up the mountain to the lush alpine pastures in the summer, once the snow has melted, but return to the lower slopes, or even the valleys in winter. Other animals hibernate to avoid the winter cold.

On the roof of the world
Because of the way they have adapted to mountain life, unrelated animals from different mountain areas look very alike. Similar goats and sheep, small plant-eaters, and predators live in mountain ranges all around the world.

Grazers
Many large grazing animals find food and refuge on the lush alpine pastures of mountains in the summer. Related to domestic goats, sheep, and cattle, they include the bighorn sheep and mountain goats of North America and the Barbary sheep of North Africa. They have thick, woolly coats and long, curly horns, and are remarkably agile, bounding up and down the mountain from one steep, rocky ledge to another, without slipping.

Nibblers
Small plant nibblers, such as the European marmot, the pika of Europe and Asia, and the chinchilla of South America, are found high in the mountains. They live in large family groups and make dens beneath boulders, where they are safe from big cats and birds of prey. Some of them, like the marmot, hibernate in winter. Others, like the pika, remain active, feeding on their stores of summer grass.

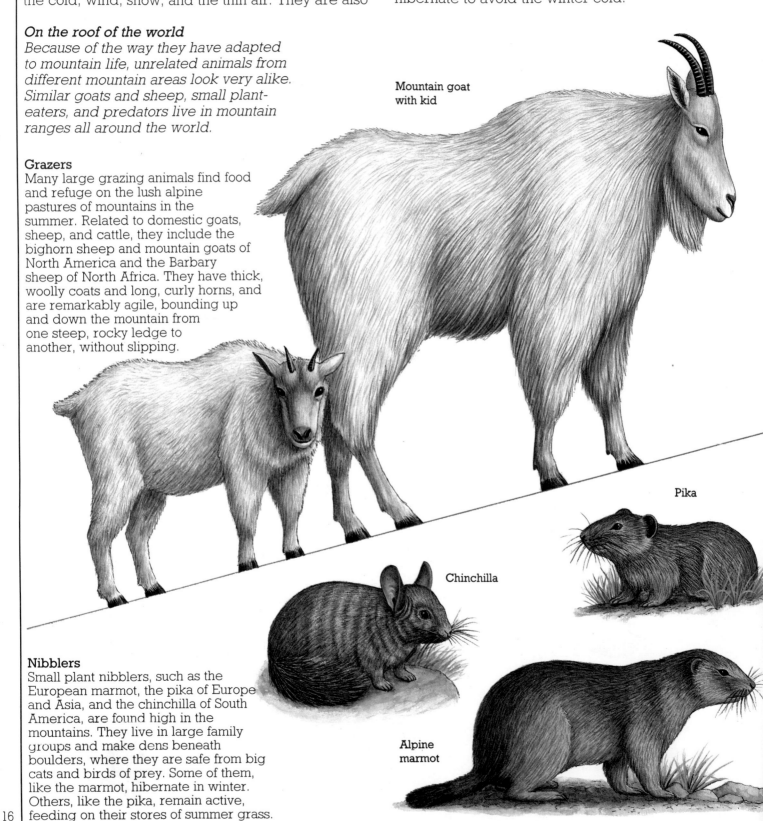

Mountain goat with kid

Pika

Chinchilla

Alpine marmot

Barbary sheep

Bighorn sheep

Lynx

Cougar

Predators
Even steep slopes cannot keep plant-eaters safe from carnivores. Big cats prey on the grazers and nibblers in most mountains. The lynx of Europe and the US, the American cougar, and the Asian snow leopard spend summer high above the tree line. Their dappled coats help to camouflage them among rocks and trees. The snow leopard has broad furry foot pads like snow shoes.

Snow leopard

LIFE ON THE WING

The most accomplished flyers of the animal world are the birds. They are not the only animals that can fly – insects and bats can, too – but the birds can fly farther and faster than any other animal. They have perfected the art of flying. They can soar in the air for hours, swoop at breakneck speeds, land on water, and perform astonishing aerobatics. Some of them can also catch their food, mate, and feed their young on the wing.

Birds are admirably suited to flying. They have powerful wings, streamlined bodies, and lots of energy. Most important of all, however, they are equipped with feathers. These are not only waterproof and warm, they also act as airfoils on birds' wings enabling them to take off and maneuver in the air. It is feathers that give the birds their unique flying ability.

The masters of the air
Here are some of the record holders among birds: those that fly the farthest, the fastest, and the highest. Each of them is uniquely adapted to the life it leads.

The longest wingspan
With a wingspan of about 10 ft (3 m), the wandering albatross has the longest wingspan of any bird. Its long, thin wings are the same shape as a glider's, and, like a glider, it can soar effortlessly over the ocean for hours once it has gained altitude.

An aerial acrobat
A master of hovering and maneuvering, the hummingbird can fly backward as well as forward and do all sorts of aerobatics. It can tilt its wings in any direction, which means that it can hover perfectly still in front of a flower, while it feeds on the nectar inside it. It flaps its wings so fast – 50 to 80 times a second – that they make the characteristic humming sound that gives it its name.

A mighty bird

The Andean condor is the heaviest bird of prey in the world, weighing up to 24 lb (11 kg). Its huge wings enable it to soar in the skies for hours, scarcely needing to flap its wings.

The great travelers

The Arctic tern is the greatest long-distance flyer among birds. It flies from the Arctic to Antarctica and back every year – a distance of about 25,000 miles (40,200 km). The sooty tern can spend 3-4 years at sea at a stretch.

Whooper swans

Arctic tern

Sooty tern

High flyers

In 1967 a flock of whooper swans was spotted by the pilot of an airplane as they were flying at a height of about 26,902 ft (8,200 m). And in 1973, a Rüppell's griffon was struck by an airplane at 37,000 ft (11,274 m) – the greatest flying height for birds ever recorded.

Flying by sonar

Bats are the only true flying mammals and they hunt at night for insects – or fruit, if they are fruit bats. Although not blind, they use a kind of sonar system to find their way and to track down prey. They make high-pitched sounds, then pick up the returning echoes, using their large, sensitive ears as receptors. In this way they can locate any object around them. Contrary to belief, most bats are clean, harmless, sociable, and highly intelligent.

Long-eared bats have especially big ears and good hearing. They are able to hover while searching for food.

The fastest seabird

The fastest flying seabird known is the magnificent frigate bird. Its wings can be up to 8 ft (2.4 m) long and enable it to fly at a top speed of 95.7 mph (154 kph).

DEEP IN THE FOREST

Across the northern parts of Europe, Asia, and North America lies a thick band of dense evergreen forest. Tall conifers, such as pine, fir, and spruce grow close together and their thickly leaved branches cut out so much light that few plants can grow beneath them. It is only in clearings or by rivers and lakes that other plants grow.

The winters are long and bitterly cold in the northern forests, and the ground is deep in snow for up to six months a year. The trees have to be tough to survive the icy cold. They have hard, waxy needles instead of leaves, and their branches slope downward, so that snow can slide off them easily.

The same types of animals live throughout the northern forests, and they too have adapted to the hard conditions and seasonal changes. Many of them hibernate during the winter or migrate to warmer feeding grounds. The animals that remain active store up food during the warm summer months to keep them going through the winter. Many of them also have coats that turn white in the winter, to help camouflage them against the snow.

The forest appears to be a dark, quiet place where nothing much is happening, but in spring and summer it comes to life.

A quiet backwater

Deep in the pine forests of North America, animals gather near a river to feed, drink, and make their nests and homes during the brief weeks of summer. Small birds and animals gather seeds from the trees and beavers are busily building a dam, while larger animals search for food to help see them through the winter.

Black bear
The black bear is very good at climbing trees. It spends every day looking for food: scooping honey from hives, collecting berries, searching for dead animals, and even fishing.

Woodpeckers
Woodpeckers are admirably suited to forest life. They nest in holes in trees and feed on insects, extracting them from the bark of the tree with their long tongues.

Hairy woodpecker

Pileated woodpecker

Spruce grouse

Nighttime creatures

The raccoon sleeps in trees during the day, but at night it looks for food along the river bank. It eats almost anything it finds, but washes its food carefully first.

The fisher is a large weasel-like animal. It lives mostly in trees and can move very fast, outrunning a squirrel. It preys on porcupines and other small animals.

An acute sense of hearing, good eyesight, a hooked bill, and sharp talons make the long-eared owl a fierce predator of small animals. Its long "ears" are really only tufts of feathers.

Crossbill
Crossbills live high in the trees and eat pine seeds. Their "crossed" bills help them to extract the seeds from the pine cones. They regurgitate them to feed to their young.

Red squirrel
The red squirrel spends its life scurrying up and down trees, using its bushy tail to help it balance. It eats huge amounts of pine seeds, leaving piles of empty pine cones behind it.

Moose
The moose is the largest deer in the world and an excellent swimmer. It spends its summers near lakes, streams, and bogs, feeding on the water plants that grow there.

Beavers
Beavers build dams across forest streams, using trees they have felled with their teeth. In the pond they build a "lodge," a dome-shaped home of sticks with underwater entrances.

Wolverine
The wolverine is the largest of all weasels and very fierce. It is extremely strong for its size and will attack almost anything. An adult can catch and kill a reindeer by itself.

Northern goshawk

Mourning cloak butterfly

Pine marten

American redstart

Yellow-rumped warbler

Moose

Beaver

Wolverine

Eastern chipmunk

Snowshoe hare
The snowshoe hare is constantly on the lookout for danger, with its large ears pricked. In summer its coat is dark brown, but as winter approaches, it turns to a snowy white.

Lynx
An agile predator with small pointed ears and a spotted coat, the lynx stalks prey like rabbits, birds or small deer. It belongs to the cat family and is a good climber.

Swallowtail
Butterflies like the swallowtail make the most of the brief summer months, drinking nectar and laying their eggs on wild flowers. They often settle near water.

Porcupine
Porcupines have strong claws which help them to climb trees in search of bark to eat. They defend themselves from predators by raising their sharp, barbed quills.

THE WORLD OF A TREE

A single tree provides food, shelter, and a hunting ground for an astonishing variety of wildlife. Owls and squirrels sleep in holes in the trunk, birds nest in the branches, spiders hide in cracks in the bark, and hundreds of insects live among the leaves.

A tree and its inhabitants form a food web. The tree makes its food from water and minerals in the soil and from sunlight. Its leaves, flowers, fruit, and even the wood itself are eaten by the insects, birds, and small mammals that live in it. These creatures are eaten by bigger animals, which in turn eventually die and disintegrate into the soil. So a tree is like a miniature world of its own.

The life of a deciduous tree, such as the oak, follows a yearly cycle. There is frantic activity in the spring and summer, when birds are feasting on the insects that are feeding on the new leaves. This is followed by a calmer period in autumn and winter. The tree loses its leaves and the animals become less active, some migrating while others hibernate.

The tree in autumn
On a mild autumn day, the golden leaves of the oak are beginning to fall. Squirrels and woodpeckers are enjoying insects and ripe acorns, and birds fly in and out of the branches of the tree, while below, the litter of dead leaves is teeming with its own animal life.

Green oak tortrix moth
The oak tortrix moth spends the day resting on the underside of an oak leaf. Oak tortrix caterpillars feed on young oak leaves in spring and can make the tree look bare.

Oak-apple and gall wasps
Oak apples are not apples: inside each one is the white larva of a gall wasp. The female lays an egg in an oak bud and the "apple" forms round the egg, protecting it while it develops.

Red admiral
The red admiral is a fast flyer and patrols a small territory of its own, chasing away intruding butterflies. It often rests and suns itself with outstretched wings.

Lesser spotted woodpecker
This bird prefers old oak trees. It works hard for hours, digging out insects from the bark. It is rarely seen, but can often be heard pecking at a rate of up to 15 times a second.

The treecreeper
This tiny brown bird runs up tree trunks, hunting for insects. Its curved bill is ideal for digging them out of the bark, and its strong claws enable it to cling tightly to the tree trunk.

Stag beetles
The larvae of these beetles live in the leaf litter beneath the oak tree. Adult males often fight each other, using their huge mandibles in the same way that stags use their antlers.

Woodlice
Woodlice live in the moist leaf litter beneath the oak tree. They would dry out in sunshine, so they are only active at night, feeding on decaying leaves, bark, and fungus.

Green woodpecker
Although it nests in a hole in the oak tree, this bird probes for insects in grass, rather than in the bark of the tree. It rarely makes the typical drumming sound of a woodpecker.

Long-tailed tit

Long-tailed tit
Long-tailed tits use their tails to help them balance on twigs in the leafy branches of the oak, while they search for insects. Their nests are balls of moss, feathers, and lichen.

Gray squirrel
The acrobatic gray squirrel scurries from tree to tree, collecting ripe acorns to eat or store for the winter. It makes a winter nest, called a drey, close to the tree trunk.

Jay

Jay
This noisy, colorful bird eats all kinds of food, even young birds. In the autumn it buries acorns in the ground and in winter it returns to its hidden food stores to feed.

Nuthatch
The nuthatch walks down the tree trunk and eats the insects the tree creeper missed. It also eats acorns, wedging them in the bark and opening them with its "hatchet" beak.

Wood pigeons
Wood pigeons may build their nests – flat platforms of twigs – in oak trees. They mainly eat farm crops and raise their young in late summer when the year's harvest is ripening.

Wood pigeons

Red admiral

Tree creeper

Wood ants
These large ants make huge nests with many tunnels from twigs and dead leaves. They prey on insects and often kill them by spraying them with formic acid.

Earwig
Earwigs are small beetle-like creatures with large pincers at the back end of their bodies. They like dark places to hide and are active at night, looking for food.

Ladybug
Not all ladybugs are black and red; some are yellow and black. They are useful to the oak tree because they eat hundreds of aphids – the insects that suck its sap – every day.

ISLAND CASTAWAYS

Some of the strangest animals in the world live on islands, where they have been cut off from mainland continents for millions of years. No two islands are the same and many of them, such as the Galapagos Islands, Madagascar, Mauritius, and Australia, have totally unique plants and animals. Some animals, though similar to others elsewhere, have grown to enormous sizes, while others are tiny (*see pages 36-37*). Some creatures look as if they haven't changed for millions of years, and others are quite unique and completely different from anything else anywhere in the world.

Island animals are unusual because thousands of years of isolation have caused them to evolve

Strange and unusual animals
Here a group of strange animals from different islands all around the world has been brought together. Each of them is unique in its own way.

Galapagos tortoise

Proboscis monkey

Giant monitor lizard

Tuatara

Giant animals
Many island animals grow larger than their relatives elsewhere. The giant monitor lizard of Komodo in Indonesia is the largest lizard in the world, being up to 10 ft (3 m) long. It is a fierce hunter.

The giant tortoises of the Galapagos Islands are truly enormous – up to 40 in (about 1 m) long. They are completely vegetarian and grow bigger as they grow older. They can live to be over 100 years old.

An unusual monkey
The odd-looking proboscis monkey is a very good swimmer and lives only on Borneo, in mangrove swamps. The male has an enormous droopy nose that it inflates to amplify its loud honking call.

A prehistoric reptile
The tuatara of New Zealand is the only survivor of a group of reptiles that lived 140 million years ago. On top of its head it has an extra eye covered with skin. No one knows why.

differently from their relatives on the mainland. These different, and sometimes strange-looking, animals have become perfectly adapted to island life, where there is little competition for food and often no predators to fear. Their isolation has made them vulnerable to interference from outside, and many of them have become extinct since being "discovered" by humans (*see pages 60-61*).

Cassowary

Red kangaroo

Platypus

Koala

Wombat

Islands of marsupials
In Australia and Tasmania there are many different kinds of marsupials. All of them rear their young in pouches. Koalas live in trees and eat nothing but eucalyptus leaves. Kangaroos roam the grasslands. They can bound along at speeds of up to 30 mph (48 kph). The wombat is an energetic digger. It lives in woods and only leaves its burrow at night to go looking for food.

An odd animal
The duckbilled platypus of Australia is very strange. It is a mammal but lays eggs. It has webbed feet and can swim and dive like an otter. It has a bill, like a duck, and a hairy coat, typical of a mammal.

Fierce and flightless
The fierce-looking cassowary of New Guinea and Australia is one of the many flightless birds to evolve on islands. It uses the bony lump on its head to push its way through the rain forests where it lives.

25

DAY AND NIGHT IN THE SHRUBLAND

In Southern Europe and around the Mediterranean, the main type of countryside is shrubland. The dry and sometimes hilly land is covered with heath and heavily scented herbs, and dotted with thorny shrubs, small evergreen oak trees, and clumps of broom. The summers here are long, hot, and very dry, and the winters are mild and wet. Any plants that grow in this dry, sun-drenched landscape have to be drought-resistant. They have long roots and tough leathery leaves that conserve moisture and help them to last for months without rain. Most of the flowers bloom briefly in the spring and early summer, before the heat of the sun shrivels them.

Many different animals live in this type of shrubland and they have also adapted to the high summer temperatures and lack of rain. Lizards and insects thrive in the heat. Frogs, toads, and snakes often bury themselves in dried-up river beds or hide under rocks to keep cool. Some butterflies rest during the hottest months of the year and only become active in the autumn. Others move to cooler areas where they can find more food.

Many animals rest during the day and only come out to feed as dusk falls and the temperature drops, so both by day and night the shrubland is constantly alive with animals. On these two pages you can see the animals that come out during the day, and on the next two pages you can see how the scene changes at night.

Golden oriole
The male golden oriole has exotic yellow and black plumage, but the female looks like a green woodpecker. Fast flyers, they dart from tree to tree. They migrate in the winter.

Wood ants
Wood ants spray powerful formic acid in the face of an attacking predator. Large colonies of wood ants can continue for several decades and have up to 300,000 worker ants.

Green woodpecker

Red squirrel

Wood ants

Black-veined white butterfly

In the heat of the day
As the sun rises high in the sky, the air becomes hot, still, and heavy with the aroma of wild herbs. Bees and wasps buzz around the sweetly scented herbs and shrubs and there is the constant humming sound of millions of grasshoppers and cicadas that are concealed in the grass and shrubs. Occasionally a lizard, which has been basking on a rock in the sun, scuttles for shelter. It looks at first as if there is nothing much to see, but really an astonishing variety of creatures live in the tough conditions of this sun-parched landscape.

Green lizard
Basking on bare earth or rocks within easy reach of a hiding place, the green lizard is alert both to danger and any insects it can eat. Only the male has the superb blue throat.

Weasel
The weasel is active both by day and night and follows a regular hunting route. It hunts rodents and rabbits, and kills them by repeatedly biting the backs of their necks.

Wild cat
The ancestor of the domestic cat, the wild cat makes its den in a hollow log among rocks and trees. Seldom seen, it hunts birds and rodents both by day and night.

Great gray shrike
An aggressive bird, the great gray shrike is also called the "butcher bird." It catches insects and lizards, then impales them on thorny bushes which it uses as a "larder."

Buzzard
The buzzard may often be seen soaring over the wooded or rocky areas where it breeds, on the lookout for small animals. As soon as it spots a victim, it swoops down on it.

Hoopoe
Named after its unusual call, "hoo-poo," this bird has an attractive plume on its head. It uses its long bill to probe the ground for insects and usually nests in a hollow tree.

Wild cat

Great gray shrike

Apollo butterfly

Rabbit

Marbled white butterfly

Stag beetle

Burnet moth

Scarce swallowtail
This butterfly flits from flower to flower in search of nectar. Its long "tails" look like antennae. This confuses attacking birds and gives the butterfly a chance to escape.

Rabbit
When grazing, rabbits have to be constantly on the lookout for predators. They have no means of defense, but they can hear well and run fast. They live together in warrens.

Honeybee
Busily searching for nectar, worker honeybees visit thousands of flowers, herbs, and trees during the summer. They take nectar back to their hive, where it is made into honey.

Argiope spider
The argiope spider spins its web over plants to ensnare butterflies and flies. The spider's bright coloring deters birds from eating it, as they think it might be poisonous.

27

Beech marten
A member of the weasel family, the beech marten is a stealthy nighttime forager and feeds on wild fruit and berries. The marten uses its bushy tail to help it balance when it climbs trees.

Barn owl
Like a phantom, the white barn owl flaps its way silently through the night, hunting for small animals and roosting birds, which it swoops upon. Its call is an eerie shriek.

Roe deer
The timid roe deer emerges from woodland at dusk to browse at the edge of the trees. If it sees any sign of danger, it gives a sharp doglike bark as a warning signal to others.

Serotine bat
Using sonar to find its prey, this large bat catches moths and beetles in its wings. Some moths are able to move out of the line of attack, as they can pick up the bat's soundwaves.

Beech marten

Roe deer

Spurge hawk moth
The caterpillars of this moth feed on poisonous plants called spurges. The bright colors of both the caterpillar and moth warn birds and lizards that they are poisonous.

Stick insect
The stick insect is hard to see as it blends in so well with grass stems and twigs. Its body, legs, and antennae are all long and thin, which helps to make it look like part of a plant.

Red fox
The fox is secretive and intelligent. It hunts by night, preying on birds and small mammals. The vixen teaches her cubs to hunt by taking them on nightly expeditions.

Smooth snake
At night, smooth snakes come out of their daytime resting places, under stones or in crevices, to feed on lizards and other small animals. They can live for up to 20 years.

Wild boar
Foraging for insects and roots, wild boars dig up the ground at twilight. They lead a solitary life, but a sow with a litter of piglets will attack fiercely if they are threatened.

Little owl
This small, flat-headed owl flies low over the shrubland at night and hunts at dusk. It bobs up and down when curious about something. Its nests in hollow trees.

A twilight world

As dusk falls, the daytime animals retire to rest and the shrubland is taken over by a completely different group of animals. Crickets take up the constant droning of the daytime grasshoppers and cicadas and there is the occasional hoot of an owl. Fireflies flash in the dark, sending messages to each other. Nocturnal caterpillars emerge to feed safely on plants, unseen by the sleeping birds. Bats flit through the sky as they leave their roosts to hunt for insects until dawn.

Many small mammals and some reptiles are active at night, foraging for their food in the undergrowth. Sharp-eyed predators, such as foxes and the silent-flying owls, leave their daytime resting places as dusk falls to hunt these nighttime creatures. Here you can see how the animals use the cover of darkness for their nocturnal activities.

Scops owl

Wild boar

Giant peacock moth

Marsh frog

Giant peacock moth
This moth has large eye markings in the center of both its upper and under wings. Their similarity to the markings on a peacock's tail gives the moth its name.

Badger
Badgers live together in groups. Active at night, they go on walks, leaving dung to mark their territory. They eat mostly earthworms in summer and roots in winter.

European tree frog
These little frogs croak loudly at night. They are more likely to be found on twigs than in water. Their shape and color help to camouflage them among the trees and shrubs.

Scorpion
A nocturnal prowler, the scorpion searches for small insects, such as earwigs and caterpillars. It stuns large prey with its stinging tail, which it arches forward over its back.

COUNTRY TO CITY

At first sight the hustle and bustle of a big city seems an unlikely place to find a wealth of wildlife. But animals have an amazing ability to adapt, changing their living and feeding habits to survive in a new environment. Blackbirds, sparrows, and mice are well-known city residents but there are many unexpected visitors, too. The animals found in cities range from raccoons and coyotes in North America, to foxes and squirrels in Europe and kangaroos in Australia.

Many animals move from the countryside to the city because their natural habitat is under threat. Trees are pulled down and undergrowth cleared to make room for new roads and houses. The city offers them shelter, food, and warmth. The large number of buildings in the city makes it warmer than the countryside, and garbage dumps provide well-stocked larders for all kinds of greedy scavengers.

The new residents

Cities provide new homes for many animals. In the search for food and security, they quickly adapt to their new surroundings.

Green corridors

A kestrel hovering above a highway is an increasingly common sight. Roads and railroad tracks form "green corridors" which lead animals into towns. Their overgrown shoulders are perfect places for animals to find food and cover without the fear of being disturbed.

In the garden

For many animals, gardens and parks offer a halfway house between country and city life. There is plenty of space and shelter and food is easy to find. Insects abound for birds to eat, and owls and foxes prey on small animals, such as mice. Animals soon change their diet, especially when people put out food for them.

Insects in the home

The countryside teems with insects, but large numbers can also be found in towns and cities.

Many, like moths and beetles, thrive in houses, feeding on food scraps, clothes, and furniture.

A common pest found in the home is the carpet beetle. Its fluffy larvae are called woolly bears. They destroy carpets by eating the woolen fibers.

The tiny holes made by adult woodworm beetles and the telltale dust from their wood-boring larvae are sure signs of this widespread pest.

The clothes moth is another pest whose larvae eat natural fibers. It lays its eggs among woolen clothes which provide food for its caterpillars.

The death watch beetle also eats wood, weakening beams and furniture. It gets its name from the eerie sound it makes as it thumps its head on the wood.

Garbage dumps

Garbage dumps are a major source of food for city animals. In North America, raccoons raid garbage cans and in Canada, polar bears have been known to venture into towns to raid garbage dumps. Scavenging gulls use discarded toothbrushes to make nests. Some animals, such as mice and rats, have become a hazard because they spread disease.

New homes

City buildings offer a wide choice of new homes for animals. Seabirds like herring gulls and oystercatchers build their nests on flat roofs instead of cliffs. House martins and swifts nest in roof eaves, storks on chimneys, and barn owls in lofts and church belfries. Bats find plenty of space and warmth in the attics of houses, which replace their homes in caves and hollow trees.

Polar bear

Raccoon

31

LIFE ON THE RIVER BANK

Some of the world's most interesting animals and plants are found in or around rivers. Every river provides water, food, and a home to a wide variety of wildlife. Throughout its length, however, a river is constantly changing. It may start its journey as a fast-moving, bubbling mountain brook, but by the time it reaches the sea it has grown much wider and calmer and flows more slowly.

Just as the river changes with each stage of its journey, so do its banks and the types of animals that live there. Water voles and kingfishers build their tunnels in the sandbanks cut away by moving water. The reed beds that grow beside slow-moving water, on the other hand, provide refuge and safe nesting places for water birds such as the grebe and reed warbler.

The river itself is a complex world of its own, teeming with microscopic creatures, insect larvae, and fish. All these provide ample food for insects patrolling the surface of the water in search of prey and for the birds and small animals that come to feed at the water's edge.

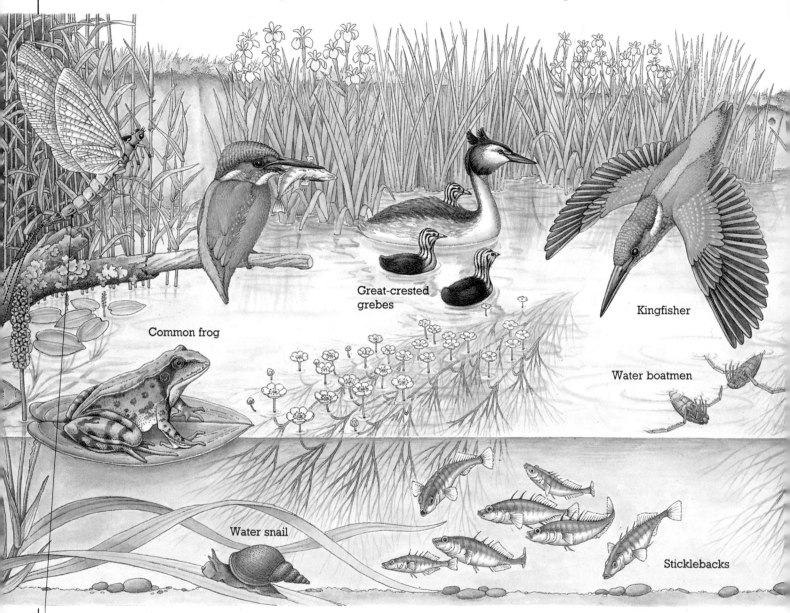

Great-crested grebes

Kingfisher

Common frog

Water boatmen

Water snail

Sticklebacks

Mayfly
Mayflies swarm at the water's edge from May onward. Their larvae live underwater for two years. The adults mate the day they are born and die the evening of the same day.

Kingfisher
The brilliant colors of the kingfisher sparkle as it dives from its perch and plunges into the water to catch fish. It lays its eggs in tunnels that it digs in the river bank.

Water boatmen
Water boatmen have strong hind legs which they use like oars to push them through the water in search of prey. They have wings too, so they are also able to fly.

Dipper
With its large, clawed feet, the dipper is an expert at walking on slippery rocks in the water. It walks upstream in fast-moving water searching for fish and crayfish to eat.

A watery world

Early summer along a quiet stretch of the river brings many animals down to the river bank. The birds are busy feeding their young and insects bask in the sunshine. The otter and kingfisher are constantly on the lookout for food.

Reed warblers

Otter

Dragonfly

Dipper

Perch

Dragonfly
Its huge eyes and four large wings make the dragonfly a fast and efficient hunter. It feeds on other insects that it catches as it flies up and down the river.

Otter
An excellent swimmer, the otter is well adapted to life in the water, with thick, waterproof fur and a long tail that it uses as a rudder. It feeds mainly on fish, but also on frogs and birds.

Water vole
This expert swimmer builds its nest in a tunnel system that it digs in the grassy bank near slow-moving water. Its burrows often have entrances both above and below water.

Caddis fly larva
Many caddis fly larvae make protective cases to live in. Some are made of pieces of stick or leaf, others out of tiny shells. Most of the larvae live and feed on the river bank.

33

MARSHLANDS

Marshlands are strange places, half land and half water. Some of them are called marshes and others bogs or swamps, but they all harbor an astonishing variety of wildlife. Some marshlands look like lakes, while others are covered in reed beds and look like grasslands, even though they are waterlogged for most of the year. There are both fresh and salt-water marshes. The freshwater ones are usually found around the edges of lakes or ponds, or where a wide river floods its banks every year. Saltwater marshes are mostly in low-lying coastal areas near a river estuary.

The Everglades in Florida look at first sight like grasslands dotted with the occasional island of trees. In fact they are a vast marshland on either side of a wide, shallow grassy river. As with many marshes, the water level in the Everglades rises and falls with the seasons, but all year round these semitropical marshes provide a home for all kinds of exotic animals.

A watery scene
The grasses, sedges, and rushes of the Everglades provide a haven for great numbers of birds which roost in the reed beds. They also form an ideal hiding place for predators such as alligators, snakes, and bobcats.

Green darner dragonfly

Everglade kite

Anhinga

Cotton mice

Largemouth bass

Blue gill

Alligator
Alligators are often found in deep pools known as "gator holes." These are always full of fish, and in the dry season many other water animals also take refuge there.

Everglade kite
Now protected in Florida, the Everglade kite has unusual feeding habits: It eats nothing but one type of water snail. It pries the snails out of their shells with its bill.

Florida turtle
Florida turtles are becoming more rare as they have been hunted by collectors. In conservation areas, they thrive in lagoons where they eat plants along the banks.

Anhinga
Anhingas dive underwater to catch fish, spearing them on their sharp beaks. They are also known as "snakebirds" because they have very long, snake-like necks.

Snowy egret
Groups of snowy egrets stand in the shallow water to feed on frogs, fish, and crayfish. With long legs and a long bill, egrets are perfectly adapted to life in the marshes.

Lilac-banded longtail
The lilac-banded longtail is purplish brown in color and prefers shade to open sunlight. This butterfly feeds on the nectar from flowers but risks being eaten by birds and lizards.

Bobcat
Bobcats are found in North America. They hunt at night for birds, rabbits, cotton mice, rats, and squirrels. They stalk their prey stealthily, then pounce on it.

Raccoon

Lilac-banded longtails

Purple gallinule

Great blue heron
The stately great blue heron stalks its prey of fish, insects, and small reptiles along the water's edge. It stands very still, then lunges at its target with its long bill.

Alligator gar
Lurking in the reed beds, the alligator gar has a long, thin body and long jaws, perfectly shaped for moving through the reeds. It is very fierce and eats most kinds of fish.

Purple gallinule
An expert at moving deftly from one floating leaf to another on its splayed-out toes, the purple gallinule feeds on seeds, fruit, leaves, and insects. It is a good swimmer.

Cottonmouth moccasin
The deadly cottonmouth moccasin snake hunts its prey at night. It swims well, holding its head above water, ready to strike at small birds, frogs, and other animals.

THE SMALLEST ANIMALS

Every branch of the animal kingdom has its midgets as well as its giants – animals that are unusually tiny and may even be too small to see with the naked eye. Nobody knows why some animals are so small. Many of them come from remote islands. Others live in dense forests where survival is perhaps easier for a small animal, which can move faster and hide more easily than a large one. The most numerous animals on Earth are in fact the smallest of all – the insects and millions of microscopic creatures too small for us to see. Here we take a look at some of the tiniest animals.

True-to-life
All the animals shown here are drawn life-size. Each one is one of the smallest animals of its type discovered so far.

A tiny primate
The lesser mouse lemur of Madagascar is one of the smallest primates (*see page 63*) in the world. It measures 12 in (30 cm) from head to tail and weighs up to 2.8 oz (80 g). It lives in dense forest and hunts for its food at night.

The smallest bird
The smallest bird in the world is the miniscule bee hummingbird, which lives in Cuba. Not much is known about it, but an adult male bird is only about 2.24 in (5.7 cm) long and half of its length is taken up with its bill and tail alone.

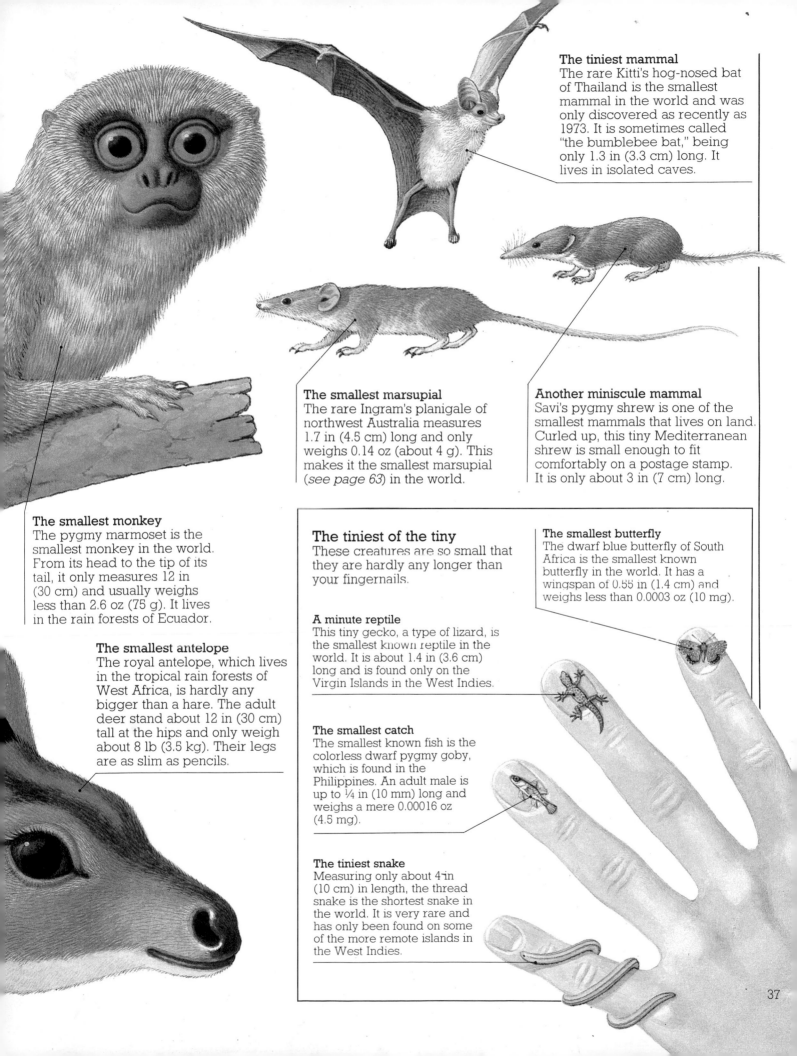

The tiniest mammal
The rare Kitti's hog-nosed bat of Thailand is the smallest mammal in the world and was only discovered as recently as 1973. It is sometimes called "the bumblebee bat," being only 1.3 in (3.3 cm) long. It lives in isolated caves.

The smallest marsupial
The rare Ingram's planigale of northwest Australia measures 1.7 in (4.5 cm) long and only weighs 0.14 oz (about 4 g). This makes it the smallest marsupial (*see page 63*) in the world.

Another miniscule mammal
Savi's pygmy shrew is one of the smallest mammals that lives on land. Curled up, this tiny Mediterranean shrew is small enough to fit comfortably on a postage stamp. It is only about 3 in (7 cm) long.

The smallest monkey
The pygmy marmoset is the smallest monkey in the world. From its head to the tip of its tail, it only measures 12 in (30 cm) and usually weighs less than 2.6 oz (75 g). It lives in the rain forests of Ecuador.

The smallest antelope
The royal antelope, which lives in the tropical rain forests of West Africa, is hardly any bigger than a hare. The adult deer stand about 12 in (30 cm) tall at the hips and only weigh about 8 lb (3.5 kg). Their legs are as slim as pencils.

The tiniest of the tiny
These creatures are so small that they are hardly any longer than your fingernails.

A minute reptile
This tiny gecko, a type of lizard, is the smallest known reptile in the world. It is about 1.4 in (3.6 cm) long and is found only on the Virgin Islands in the West Indies.

The smallest catch
The smallest known fish is the colorless dwarf pygmy goby, which is found in the Philippines. An adult male is up to ¼ in (10 mm) long and weighs a mere 0.00016 oz (4.5 mg).

The tiniest snake
Measuring only about 4 in (10 cm) in length, the thread snake is the shortest snake in the world. It is very rare and has only been found on some of the more remote islands in the West Indies.

The smallest butterfly
The dwarf blue butterfly of South Africa is the smallest known butterfly in the world. It has a wingspan of 0.55 in (1.4 cm) and weighs less than 0.0003 oz (10 mg).

THE GREAT GRASSLANDS

More than a quarter of all the land on Earth is covered in grass, and most of the continents have vast grasslands that spread for thousands of miles. Different countries have different names for their grasslands. In North America they are called plains and prairies and in South America, the pampas. In Central Asia there are steppes, and the grassy plains of East Africa are called savannahs.

The great grasslands of the world are all in areas where few trees grow, either because there is not enough rain for them or because the ground is too dry and sandy. Grasses are very tough. They carry on growing after flood, fire, or drought and can withstand constant grazing by animals. Because of this, they provide a continuous food supply for great numbers of plant-eating animals, many of which have become especially adapted to feeding on them. Here, and on the next two pages you can see some of the animals, both large and small, that live on the wide plains of the African savannah.

The savannah of East Africa

On the savannah, seas of open grassland are dotted with the occasional thorn bush and acacia tree. More groups of large mammals live on these grassy plains than anywhere else in the world.

Lions

Lions live in groups called prides, led by a dominant male. Most of the hunting is done by lionesses, often as a team. They chase victims into an ambush set by other members of the pride.

Hyenas

Hyenas are ferocious meat-eaters which hunt at night in packs. They single out a victim from a herd of wildebeest or zebra and chase it until it tires, then attack it.

Giraffe

The giraffe's enormous height enables it to eat the leaves at the tops of trees which other browsing animals cannot reach, so it usually has a plentiful supply of food.

Elephants

Herds of elephants move slowly across the savannah, browsing and grazing. In the dry season they often travel or "migrate" long distances in search of fresh pastures.

Hyenas

Vultures

Vultures

Vultures soar at great heights above the African plains, searching for an abandoned kill. Once they have sighted a carcass they land in droves to feed on the remains.

Eland

Many types of antelope roam the savannah. The eland is the largest of them. Like other antelopes and hooved animals, they graze in large herds, seeking safety in numbers.

Wildebeest

Wildebeest live in huge herds, often several thousand strong. The whole herd migrates vast distances when the dry season starts, in search of water and fresh pastures.

Weaver bird colonies

Because trees on the savannah are scattered, whole flocks of gregarious weaver birds weave their elaborate basket-shaped nests in the same thorn bush or tree.

Weaver birds

Wildebeest

Zebras

Leopard

Thomson's gazelle

Zebras

Zebras live in herds, often close to wildebeest. Their main enemy is the lion, and some people think the zebra's stripes help to confuse lions when they give chase.

Thomson's gazelle

The Thomson's gazelle is more numerous than any other gazelle on the savannah. When being pursued by a predator, it twists and turns to try and escape its attacker.

Rhinoceros

There are two types of African rhino – the black one, which feeds on leaves and twigs, and the white one, which eats mainly grass. The rhino uses its horns to defend itself.

Leopard

The leopard hunts on its own and its spots help to camouflage it as it stalks its prey. It uses a tree as its "pantry," carrying its kill up on to a branch, out of reach of scavengers.

Forest of grass

A closer look at the savannah scene on the previous pages reveals another, hidden world of animals. Among the tall clumps of grass and plants live birds, lizards, snakes, and thousands of tiny scurrying insects. To these animals, the stalks of grass are like a tall, dense forest where they live, breed and take refuge.

Zebra

Secretary bird

Banded mongoose

Ants

Banded mongoose

The mongoose is a formidable snake-killer. It relies on its speed and agility to avoid a snake's poisonous fangs. Mongooses also eat birds' eggs, lizards, and small mammals.

Common agama

This small lizard lives in groups of up to 25 members and forages for insects like grasshoppers and locusts. The female lays her eggs in the warm soil in the rainy season.

Grasshopper

The grasshopper is one of the most common grassland insects and is eaten by many other animals. It uses its long back legs to leap away from danger.

Puff adder

The puff adder is one of the grasslands' most dangerous predators. Camouflaged among the grass, it lies in wait for its prey and strikes with its long, poisonous fangs.

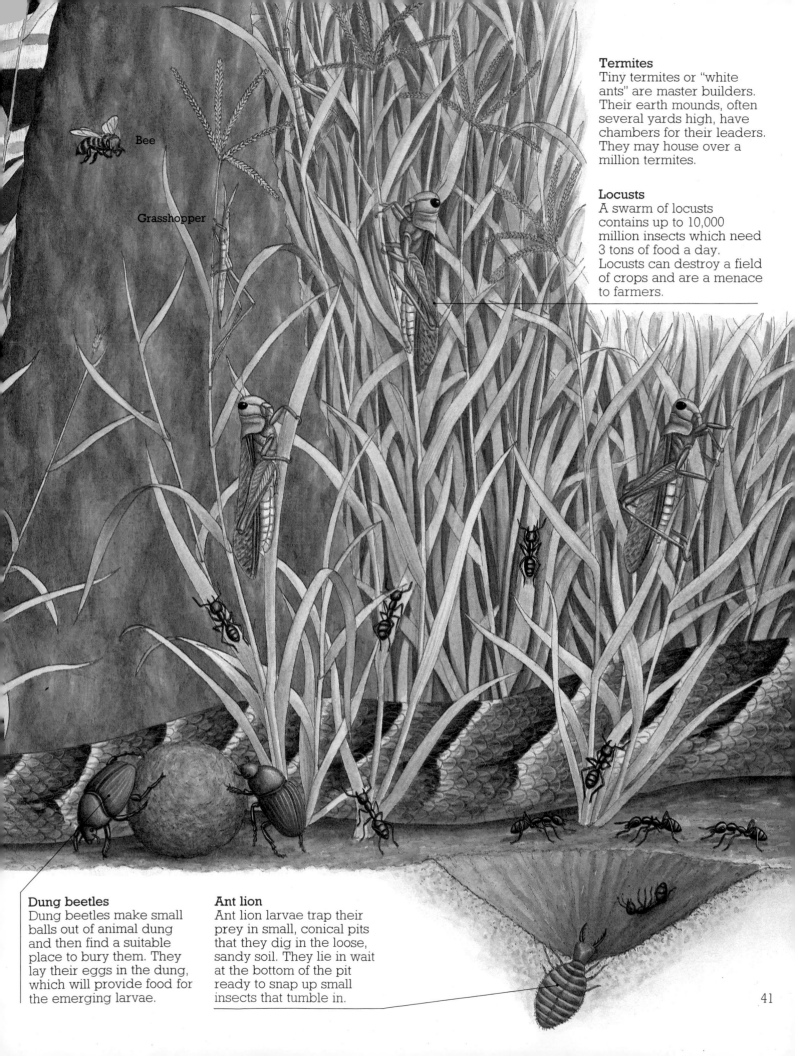

Bee

Grasshopper

Termites
Tiny termites or "white ants" are master builders. Their earth mounds, often several yards high, have chambers for their leaders. They may house over a million termites.

Locusts
A swarm of locusts contains up to 10,000 million insects which need 3 tons of food a day. Locusts can destroy a field of crops and are a menace to farmers.

Dung beetles
Dung beetles make small balls out of animal dung and then find a suitable place to bury them. They lay their eggs in the dung, which will provide food for the emerging larvae.

Ant lion
Ant lion larvae trap their prey in small, conical pits that they dig in the loose, sandy soil. They lie in wait at the bottom of the pit ready to snap up small insects that tumble in.

41

HUNTERS AND THE HUNTED

All animals need a regular supply of food. Plant-eaters have to eat a lot and spend most of their time grazing and browsing. When they have eaten all the food in one area, they move on to another. Meat-eaters eat other animals, so they have to be efficient hunters to survive. The animals they hunt, however, have to be able to fend them off or to escape, so that *they* survive. The relationship between the hunter and the hunted is constantly changing. Sometimes the hunter wins and catches its prey; at other times the prey manages to escape from the hunter. Every predator has its own method of hunting. Some hunt on their own and others in packs. Some chase their victims, others ambush them or lay traps for them. The animals they hunt use all kinds of tricks to confuse their enemies, as they are often unable to defend themselves. Here you can find out about some of the widely varying techniques of attack and defense carried out by the hunters and the animals they hunt.

A swift-footed hunter
A cheetah springs forward into a herd of wildebeest. They flee in all directions, twisting, turning, and kicking, in an attempt to confuse their pursuer and throw it off track.

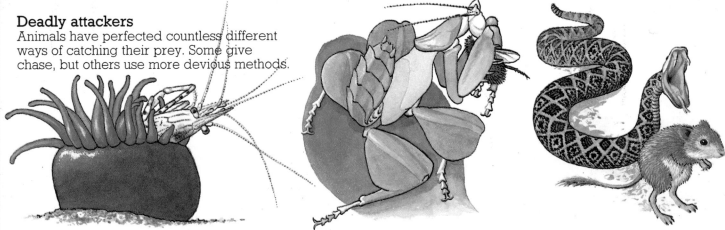

Deadly attackers
Animals have perfected countless different ways of catching their prey. Some give chase, but others use more devious methods.

Stinging tentacles
The sea anemone stuns its prey with its stinging, poisonous tentacles. Its tentacles then close around the paralyzed prey and draw it down into the sea anemone's mouth.

A deadly disguise
This mantis is exactly the same color as the flower on which it is sitting. Perfectly camouflaged, it lies in wait of unsuspecting insects that visit the flower.

Poisonous fangs
The rattlesnake has needle-sharp, poisonous fangs. When it senses prey, it glides silently forward, then strikes swiftly, sinking its fangs deep into its victim.

Keeping watch
Wildebeest seek safety in numbers by moving around in vast herds. They keep a constant lookout for danger as they graze on the savannah, frequently lifting their heads to look around. It is hard for a predator to creep up on them unseen.

The hunter
The cheetah relies on its speed to catch prey and can run at up to 60 mph (100 kph) over short distances. It selects an animal from a herd, then creeps up as close as possible to its victim and suddenly sprints forward at lightning speed.

The chase
The herd scatters, but the cheetah pursues its victim. Unable to run at high speed for long, the cheetah only catches its prey if it can keep up with it for the first few hundred yards. It then brings the animal down and bites its throat to kill it.

Avoiding tactics
Not all animals run away from their predators. Some try to frighten attackers away and others use tricks to bluff the enemy.

Faking injury
The ringed plover leads predators away from its young by pretending to have a broken wing and moving away from its nest. A safe distance away, it flies up and escapes.

All puffed up
When threatened, the puffer fish swallows water so that it looks twice its normal size. Its body swells into a balloon shape and all its spines stick out, frightening off its enemy.

Threatening behavior
The frilled lizard of Australia tries to frighten off attackers by hissing and spreading its huge, frilled "collar," to make it look bigger and more fierce than it really is.

43

THE STEAMING JUNGLE

Rain forests, or jungles, are dense, steamy forests that grow in the tropics near the Equator, where it is very hot and rains nearly every day.

The trees and plants grow very fast, competing with each other for light, and reach enormous heights, spreading out their branches and leaves like green parasols at the top. Ordinary plants grow to the size of trees and the trees themselves are among the tallest in the world. There is very little seasonal change in the jungle.

Jungles harbor the greatest variety of plants and animals in the world. These live at different levels in the trees, as in a multistory building, each level being completely different from the others. The forest floor is mostly dark and gloomy. It is very hot and the air is still. Higher up, creepers called lianas hang in thick ropes between the towering tree trunks. Most of the animals in the jungle live right at the top of the trees, about 150 ft (45 m) above the ground, in the "canopy," where there is plenty of sunlight and leaves, flowers, and fruit to feed on. On these two pages you can see the animals that live at ground level in the Amazon jungle of South America, the largest jungle in the world, and on the next two pages you can discover what life is like up in the canopy, high in the treetops.

Deep in the Amazon

The Amazon jungle is intersected by the Amazon River and thousands of smaller rivers. Shafts of sunlight reach the ground where a river breaks the wall of trees. Many reptiles and fish live in the murky waters and other birds and animals come to feed and drink at the water's edge.

Anteater
Anteaters feed on termites and ants. They rip open the nests of their prey with their long, powerful claws, and lick up the insects with their 2 ft (60 cm) tongues, coated in sticky saliva.

Black caiman
Caimans are relatives of the alligator. They live close to the river, snapping up unwary small animals and birds which come to drink at the water's edge. They can lay up to 30 eggs at a time.

Anaconda
The largest living snake, the anaconda attacks birds and animals that come to the river to drink. It winds its body around its prey, squeezes it to death, then swallows it whole.

Arrau turtle
The Arrau turtle is one of the largest freshwater turtles. The heavy female turtles haul themselves out onto the sandbanks to lay their eggs. They can lay up to 150 eggs each year.

Hatchet fish

Neon tetra fish

Electric eel

Manatee
The timid manatee or sea-cow rests under the water by day, only rising to breathe. It feeds on plants, tearing them up from the river bed with its strong upper lip.

Army ants

Morpho butterflies

44

Hoatzin
The odd-looking hoatzin is not very good at flying and prefers to clamber around trees. The baby birds have claws on their wings to help them grip on to branches as they climb trees.

Scarlet ibis

Arrau turtle

Arapaima

Hatchet fish
The hatchet fish of the Amazon are the world's only true flying fish. They can actually flap their outstretched fins and "fly" above the water in pursuit of airborne insects.

Capybara
Capybara are the largest rodents (*see page 63*) on Earth – the size of pigs. Their feet are partially webbed. They spend most of their time in the river, feeding on plants.

Piranhas
Very ferocious, piranhas hunt in shoals of several hundred. They tear the flesh from their prey with their sharp teeth. Strangely, some types of piranha only eat plants.

Jaguar
The mottled coat of the jaguar camouflages it as it stalks its prey through the dimly lit trees. It is the largest cat in South America and is able to climb trees and swim.

The treetop canopy

Unlike woodland trees, jungle trees have no branches low down. They start branching about 100 ft (30 m) from the ground, providing a dense canopy of branches and leaves. This tangled world of trees, orchids, ferns, and other plants is home to a wide variety of insects, snakes, animals, and birds who are able to live high above the ground. Birds, monkeys, and sloths grip tightly to the branches, as they forage for luscious fruits, flowers, leaves, and berries.

Howler monkey

Feeding by day on leaves and fruit, howler monkeys move deftly through the canopy. The males loudly defend their territory – their roaring voices can be heard 2 miles (3 km) away.

Sloth

Living and sleeping upside down, the sloth has hook-like claws that cling on tightly as it inches its way slowly along the branches of a tree. It feeds on leaves and buds.

Tree boa

Sloth

Tree porcupine

Tree porcupine

The tree porcupine uses its tail, as well as its feet, to help it grip branches tightly. Despite its protective quills, the porcupine is preyed on by eagles.

Tree boa
Hidden in the leaves, the emerald tree boa camouflages itself by pressing its body close to the branch. It strikes at its prey to catch it, then squeezes it to death.

Harpy eagle
Harpy eagles are the feared predators of the canopy. They chase their prey at speeds of 50 mph (80 kph), and pluck monkeys from branches with their massive claws.

Spider monkey
The most agile of monkeys, spider monkeys swing from branch to branch through the canopy. They use their long and very strong tails to grip the branches.

Toucan
When asleep, a toucan lays its rainbow-colored bill along its back and covers the bill with its tail. It uses its incredible bill to pick fruit and berries and toss them down its throat.

Frilled coquette hummingbird

Ruby topaz hummingbird

Macaw
Macaws are the largest of the South American parrots. They have vice-like feet for gripping branches and strong hooked beaks for cracking open nuts to eat.

Butterflies
There is a greater variety of butterflies in the jungle than anywhere else in the world. Their dazzling colors help to camouflage them when they alight on brightly colored flowers.

Hummingbird
Glossy hummingbirds hover in front of flowers as if suspended in midair. They probe inside the flowers for nectar with their long tongues, pollinating them as they do so.

Tree frog
A huge variety of tree frogs spend their entire lives high in the trees. Some live in the water that collects in the center of plants growing on lofty tree branches.

CAMOUFLAGE AND SIGNALING

All animals have a strong natural instinct for survival and many of them have adapted to their habitats in very clever ways. Many animals need to be as inconspicuous as possible most of the time, so that they are not spotted by hungry predators. Constantly running away or looking for hiding places takes up a lot of time, so some animals have developed cunning forms of camouflage, which make them very hard to see. The colors and patterns of their coats, feathers, or skin match the color of their surroundings so well that they become almost invisible.

Camouflage is not the only way in which animals make use of color and pattern. Some animals are brilliantly colored and actually show off their colors as much as possible, even to their enemies. Their bright colors are used to proclaim who they are, flaunted as a challenge to other males, and shown off to attract a mate. Sometimes certain combinations of bright colors, such as yellow and black, or red and black, show that an animal is poisonous and should be avoided.

Color and pattern are both used as a means of signaling, but animals have other ways of passing on messages to each other, too. Here you can find out more types of camouflage and signaling in the animal world.

Showing off
Male birds use all sorts of tricks to attract a mate. Many of them are brilliantly colored and show off their feathers or perform elaborate courtship dances to win a female's attention.

Frigate birds

Camouflage artists
Animal camouflage can take many forms. One of the most common is for an animal to have a mottled coat or feathers with patches of dark and light coloring. This makes it hard to see against a background of rocks or sun-dappled foliage, especially when it keeps still. Other animals, such as some insects, look like part of the plant on which they live. One of the best camouflage artists of all is the chameleon, a type of lizard, which constantly changes color to match its surroundings.

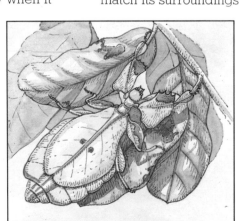

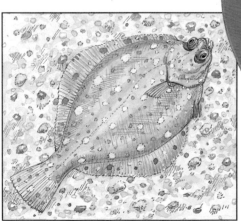

The Texas horned lizard matches the stony desert ground on which it lives so well that when it stands still it is almost invisible. Its camouflage enables it to lie in wait for unsuspecting birds and small animals that come too close, then attack them.

The leaf insects of the tropics mimic the color and the shape of the leaves among which they live. They do this so successfully that they would never be able to move to another type of plant, as they would be spotted by a predator instantly.

The flounder is very hard to detect as it lies on the sea bed. It can change its color and pattern to match its background perfectly. Its body is flattened out to hug the surface of the sand or rocks it lies on, so both its eyes are on the top side of its head.

A dazzling display
The male birds of paradise of Papua New Guinea perform courtship dances on a tree branch to win a mate. The drab-looking females choose the males with the most dazzling plumage and dance.

Birds of paradise

Passing on messages
Animals do not always communicate with each other by sound. They can pass messages to each other by means of color and behavior.

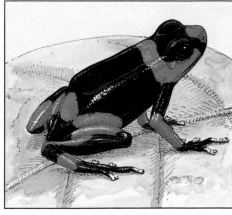

The ring-tailed lemurs of Madagascar spend almost as much time on the ground as they do in the trees. They signal each other by waving their long, banded black and white tails, which give off odors from their scent glands.

The spectacular colors of this South American frog warn potential predators that it is highly poisonous. The poison that the frog secretes in slime from its skin is lethal enough to paralyze a bird or a small monkey within minutes.

A courtship dance
Gannets always recognize each other in the crowded colonies where they live, because each one has slightly different markings. Courting pairs perform dances where each movement and step has a special meaning.

Macaw

Gannets

Lorikeet

A magnificent chest
During courtship, the male frigate bird tries to impress the female by inflating his bright scarlet throat pouch into a kind of balloon. The female shows her interest in him by rubbing her head against his spectacular chest.

Gaudy birds
The macaws of South America and the lorikeets of Australia, New Zealand, and the Pacific Islands live in noisy flocks high up in the rain forests. Their brilliant colors help them to recognize each other.

49

THE BURNING DESERT

Deserts are the driest places on Earth. In parts of them it may not rain for many years. Some deserts are vast expanses of sand. Others are rocky or covered in thin scrub. Some of them, like the Gobi desert in Asia, are cold in the winter, but many of them are hot year-round. Temperatures soar to great heights during the day but may often drop to well below freezing at night.

Deserts often look dead, as if nothing grows or lives there, but many amazing plants and animals have adapted to life in the harsh conditions. Desert plants have long roots and tough skins. They flower and seed the moment there is rain. Desert animals have unique ways of coping without much water. On the next four pages you can find out about life in two different kinds of desert.

The biggest desert on Earth
The Sahara stretches right across northern Africa. Most of the animals that live there shelter from the burning heat during the day and only emerge to hunt for food as the sun sinks in the sky.

Surviving the desert
These three desert animals have developed especially clever ways of coping with the intense heat and lack of water.

Dromedary camel
The camel is the largest animal in the desert. It can survive for weeks without water, living on the food reserves stored as fat in its hump and on water that it stores in its stomach. It can cope with intense heat, as its large body heats up slowly and it does not have to sweat much to keep cool. Its feet splay out as it walks, so that they do not sink into the sand, and during sandstorms it can close its nostrils to keep out sand.

Lanner falcon
The lanner falcon soars over the desert by day, searching for small animals to eat. It swoops down on its prey, seizing it in its sharp talons, and tears it apart with its hooked beak.

Gecko
The gecko is a type of lizard that can skim across the sand. It has webbed toes that stop it from sinking. It uses its toes like shovels to help burrow beneath the sand.

Gerbil
The hopping, mouselike gerbil ventures from its burrow at dusk to feed. It gets all the liquid it needs from the seeds and grasses it eats, and is hunted by the fennec fox.

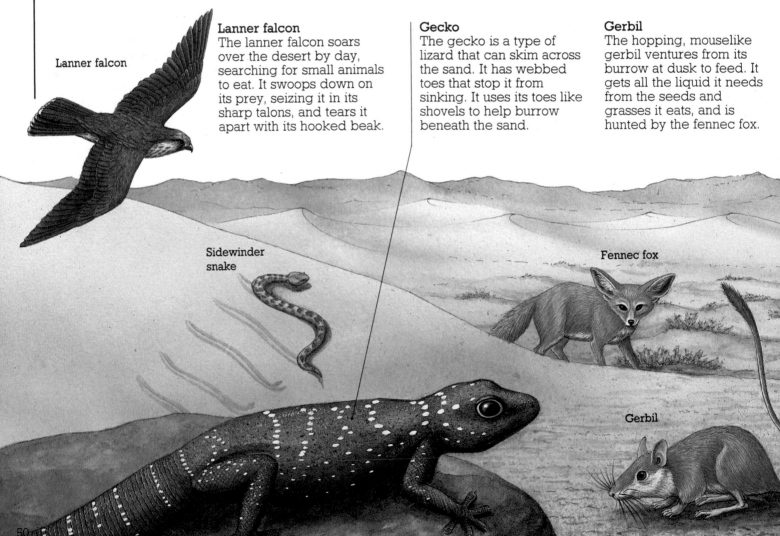

Lanner falcon

Sidewinder snake

Fennec fox

Gerbil

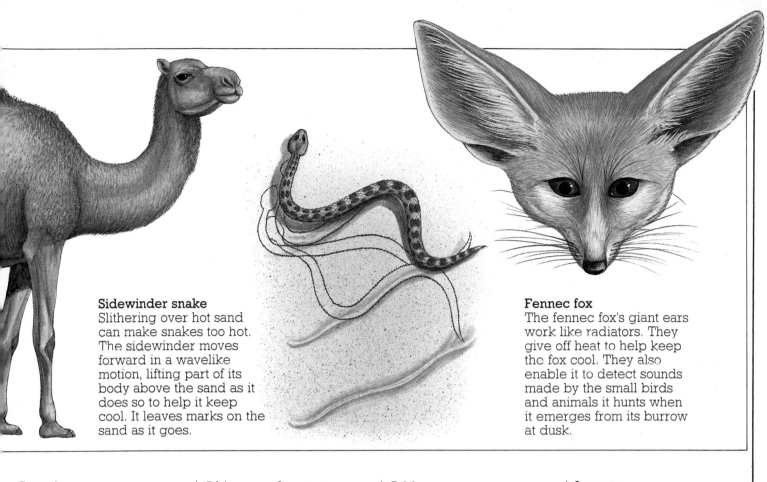

Sidewinder snake
Slithering over hot sand can make snakes too hot. The sidewinder moves forward in a wavelike motion, lifting part of its body above the sand as it does so to help it keep cool. It leaves marks on the sand as it goes.

Fennec fox
The fennec fox's giant ears work like radiators. They give off heat to help keep the fox cool. They also enable it to detect sounds made by the small birds and animals it hunts when it emerges from its burrow at dusk.

Scorpion
Scorpions mainly use the venomous stingers in their tails to defend themselves. They catch insects and spiders in their giant pincers, then tear them apart to eat.

African sand grouse
The sand grouse flies great distances to the nearest waterhole to get water for its chicks. It soaks its breast feathers, then flies back to its chicks which suck the water out.

Addax
The addax antelope has wide hooves that help it to move easily across the sand. It does not drink water at all but gets all the liquid it needs from the plants it eats.

Locusts
Locusts are desert relatives of grasshoppers that lay their eggs in warm sand. They swarm in millions, eating thousands of tons of plants before moving on to a new area.

Scorpion

THE NORTH AMERICAN DESERT

The North American deserts lie in the southwest part of the United States. Here the summers are hot and the winters are cold – snow may even fall. These deserts are not sandy landscapes with huge dunes. Parts of them are stony and bare, dotted with rocks and hills that have been worn into strange shapes by the wind. Other areas are covered in low-lying scrub and thorn bushes.

The best known of the American desert plants are the cacti. Like many other desert plants, they can store water. When it rains, their widespread roots suck up water and their stems swell to store it. Other plants also come to life when it rains. Seeds that may have been lying dormant for years suddenly sprout, flower, and make new seeds, briefly turning the desert into a meadow.

The desert at night

As night falls, the desert comes to life. Kangaroo rats emerge from their burrows, and spiders and scorpions appear from beneath rocks, as all the animals start their search for food.

Adapting to life in the desert

Each of these three animals has its own way of avoiding the heat and conserving liquid in the harsh desert conditions.

Kangaroo rat

The kangaroo rat keeps cool during the day by staying in its burrow, the mouth of which it plugs up to keep the air inside cool and moist. Like the gerbil of the Sahara, it gets all the liquid it needs from the seeds it eats.

Poor-will

The poor-will's coloring helps to camouflage it in rocky areas. It avoids the bitter cold of the winter by hibernating, waking in spring when there are more insects to eat.

Rattlesnake

The rattlesnake is poisonous and shakes the rattle on its tail as a warning if a big animal comes too near. It hunts small animals, killing them with its poisonous fangs.

Chuckwalla

The chuckwalla lizard hides under a rock during the night and comes out to bask in the sun in the morning. A plant-eater, this lizard stores water in folds of skin on its sides.

Gila monster

This bulky lizard is poisonous, and its bright colors act as a warning to predators. It eats birds and lizard eggs and stores fat in its thick tail for times of food shortage.

Jack rabbit

Coyote

Gila monster

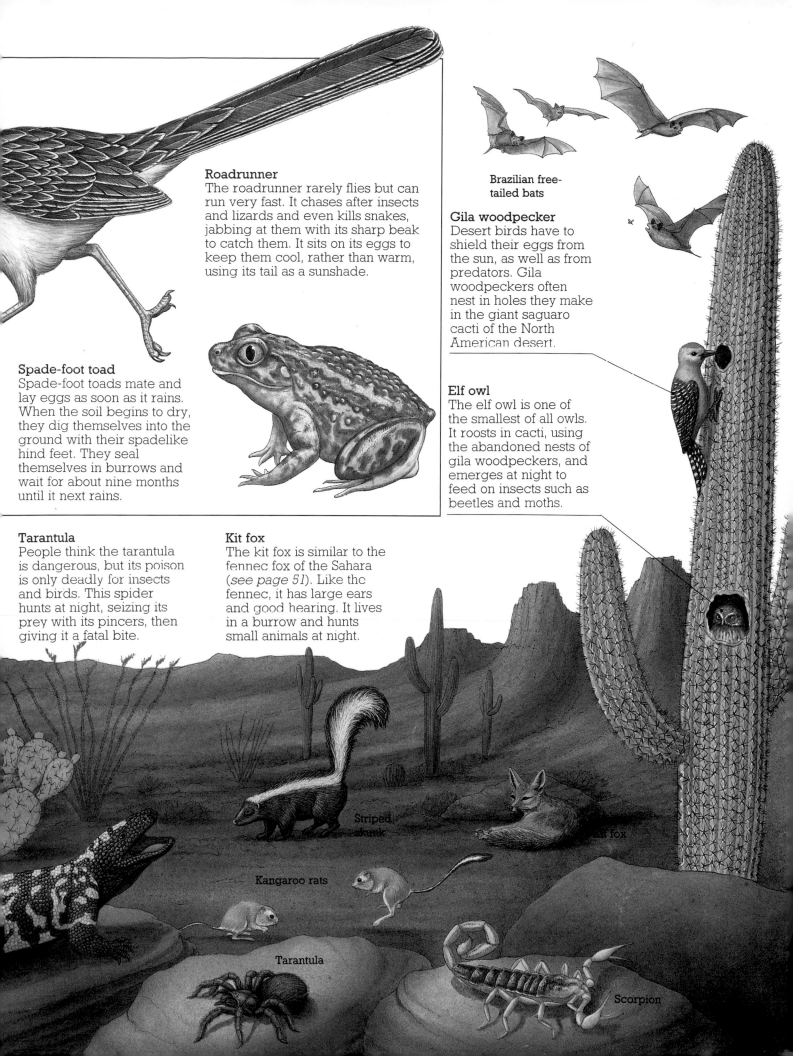

Roadrunner
The roadrunner rarely flies but can run very fast. It chases after insects and lizards and even kills snakes, jabbing at them with its sharp beak to catch them. It sits on its eggs to keep them cool, rather than warm, using its tail as a sunshade.

Spade-foot toad
Spade-foot toads mate and lay eggs as soon as it rains. When the soil begins to dry, they dig themselves into the ground with their spadelike hind feet. They seal themselves in burrows and wait for about nine months until it next rains.

Tarantula
People think the tarantula is dangerous, but its poison is only deadly for insects and birds. This spider hunts at night, seizing its prey with its pincers, then giving it a fatal bite.

Kit fox
The kit fox is similar to the fennec fox of the Sahara (*see page 51*). Like the fennec, it has large ears and good hearing. It lives in a burrow and hunts small animals at night.

Brazilian free-tailed bats

Gila woodpecker
Desert birds have to shield their eggs from the sun, as well as from predators. Gila woodpeckers often nest in holes they make in the giant saguaro cacti of the North American desert.

Elf owl
The elf owl is one of the smallest of all owls. It roosts in cacti, using the abandoned nests of gila woodpeckers, and emerges at night to feed on insects such as beetles and moths.

Striped skunk

Kit fox

Kangaroo rats

Tarantula

Scorpion

THE BURROWERS

Not all animals spend their lives out in the open. Some of them dig burrows and spend part or all of their time underground, where predators cannot reach them and they can bring up their young safely. A burrow can provide protection from the sun in hot places or a sheltered spot to hibernate in cold places. They may be dug in soil, sand, or snow. Some burrowers live almost permanently underground; others just use their burrow as a retreat. Most burrowing animals have thick, warm fur, strong claws for digging, and streamlined bodies so they can move easily under the ground.

Badgers
With strong front claws and powerful bodies, badgers are well-designed for burrowing. Their dens, which are usually no more than 6 ft (2 m) below ground, may be used by different badgers for centuries.

Moles
Moles are master burrowers, using their large front paws like spades. They are very shortsighted but have whiskers on their faces for feeling their way underground.

Earthworms
As many as 500 worms may live in one square yard of soil. They make their tunnels by pushing and eating their way through the soil. Tiny hairs on their bodies stop them from slipping as they dig.

Burrowing owl
Empty prairie dog burrows are often used as nests by the burrowing owls of the American prairies. The owls use their large claws to make the holes bigger, and feed their young on insects.

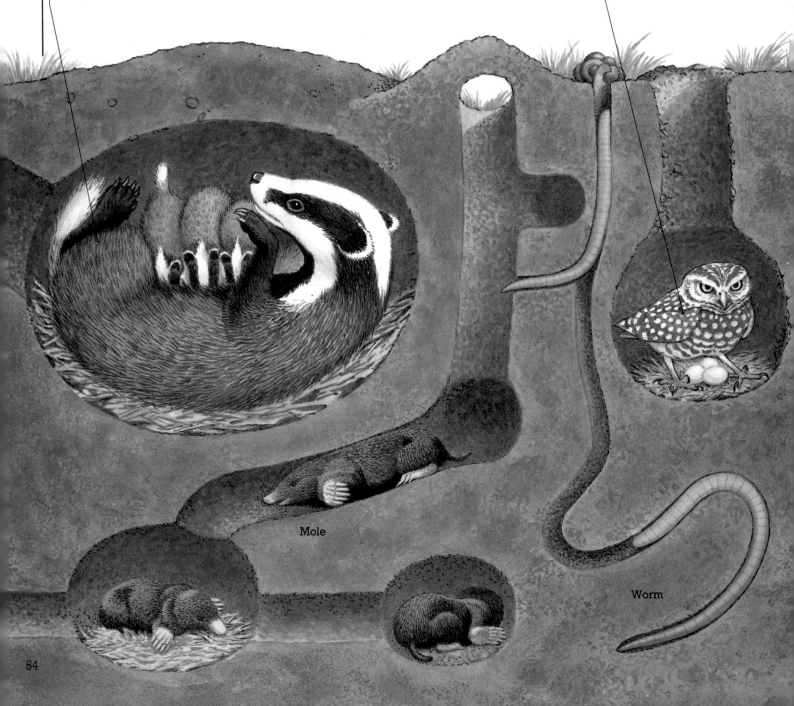

Mole

Worm

Life underground

Here you can see different burrowers in their homes. All of them burrow in soil, but you would never normally find them together as they come from different places all around the world.

Pink fairy armadillo
This South American armadillo spends most of its life underground. It only ventures outside at night to hunt for insects. It makes its burrow by digging with its front legs and pushing with its snout.

Rabbits
A large rabbit warren may house 400 rabbits and have over 2,000 entrances. Different tunnels act as roadways, bedrooms, and nurseries. Rabbits also use small burrows and even old foxes' dens as homes.

Prairie dogs
Several thousand prairie dogs may live together as a "township." If there is danger, they let out high-pitched barks to warn the others to dive underground.

Trapdoor spider
The trapdoor spider digs a deep tunnel in the soil and covers the entrance with a fine silk web and moss. As an unsuspecting insect walks across it, the spider lifts up its trapdoor and grabs its prey.

Prairie dogs

Rabbits

55

THE OCEAN DEPTHS

The seas and oceans are the largest natural habitat, covering over two thirds of the Earth. The oceans are vast and varied. The sea bed has a landscape more dramatic than dry land, with towering mountains and deep, dark chasms. In places the mountains are so high that they form islands above the surface of the water. The oceans are, however, still mostly unknown. They are among the last places left on Earth that humans have not really explored and there are probably many animals living there yet to be discovered.

A huge variety of creatures live in the oceans, varying in size from microscopic plankton to the blue whale. Most animals live in the sunlit surface waters of the sea, where plant food is plentiful. This is grazed by large shoals of small fish that are hunted in turn by larger fish. Several miles below, however, the waters are pitch dark and freezing cold. No plants can grow at this depth, yet numerous strange fish flourish there, many of them providing their own light with a weird array of luminous spines and fins.

A world on different levels

This imaginary scene shows some of the animals that live at different levels in the ocean – from the shoals of small fish that live in the warm surface waters to the grotesque-looking creatures that lurk in the murky depths far below.

Man-of-war
Beneath its float, which acts like a sail, the Portuguese man-of-war trails deadly stinging tentacles through the water. These paralyze and kill unsuspecting fish that swim into them.

Tuna
With streamlined bodies and forked tails, tuna are high-speed swimmers that travel great distances. Their main source of food is squid and smaller fish.

Squid
Squid are very fast swimmers and move forward and backward with equal ease. They have a horny beak and ten tentacles with suckers. Giant squid have the largest known eyes of any animal in the world.

A world in miniature

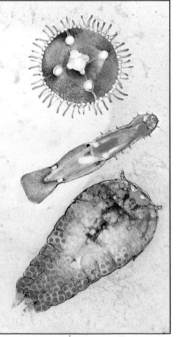

The seas are full of tiny drifting plants called *phytoplankton*. These are an astonishing variety of shapes, but they are so small they can only be seen under a microscope. Most of them live in the top 330 ft (100 m) of water, where sunlight can reach them and they can grow. Feeding on these tiny plants are miniscule drifting creatures called *zooplankton*. The two types of plankton are the main food supply of many sea creatures. Even the blue whale feeds on some types of plankton, sieving it from the water.

Hatchet fish
These tiny deep-sea fish have transparent fins and telescopic eyes that point upward. Their bodies are flattened from side to side and they have rows of lights on their undersides.

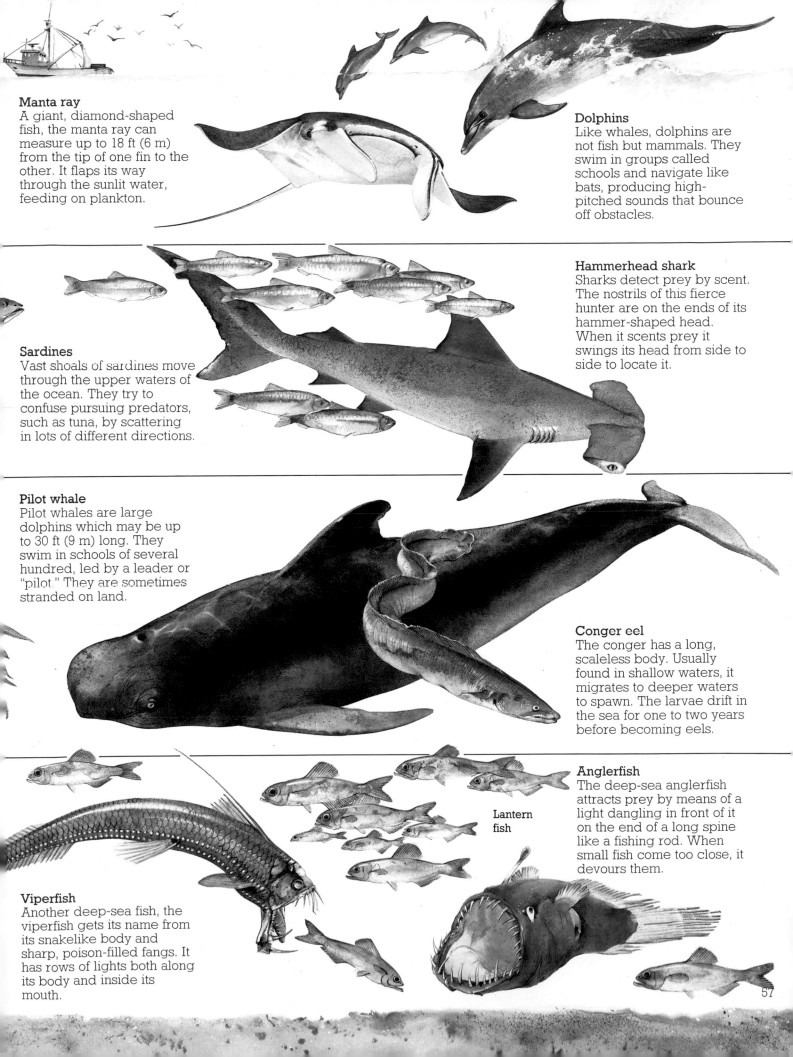

Manta ray
A giant, diamond-shaped fish, the manta ray can measure up to 18 ft (6 m) from the tip of one fin to the other. It flaps its way through the sunlit water, feeding on plankton.

Dolphins
Like whales, dolphins are not fish but mammals. They swim in groups called schools and navigate like bats, producing high-pitched sounds that bounce off obstacles.

Sardines
Vast shoals of sardines move through the upper waters of the ocean. They try to confuse pursuing predators, such as tuna, by scattering in lots of different directions.

Hammerhead shark
Sharks detect prey by scent. The nostrils of this fierce hunter are on the ends of its hammer-shaped head. When it scents prey it swings its head from side to side to locate it.

Pilot whale
Pilot whales are large dolphins which may be up to 30 ft (9 m) long. They swim in schools of several hundred, led by a leader or "pilot." They are sometimes stranded on land.

Conger eel
The conger has a long, scaleless body. Usually found in shallow waters, it migrates to deeper waters to spawn. The larvae drift in the sea for one to two years before becoming eels.

Anglerfish
The deep-sea anglerfish attracts prey by means of a light dangling in front of it on the end of a long spine like a fishing rod. When small fish come too close, it devours them.

Lantern fish

Viperfish
Another deep-sea fish, the viperfish gets its name from its snakelike body and sharp, poison-filled fangs. It has rows of lights both along its body and inside its mouth.

THE LIFE OF THE CORAL REEF

Coral reefs are one of the wonders of the natural world, forming brilliantly colored underwater kingdoms inhabited by vast numbers of exotic creatures and plants. They only grow in warm tropical waters shallow enough for the sun to reach them. Muddy or polluted water kills them.

The reefs take thousands of years to form and are built entirely by tiny creatures no more than a half-inch long. These creatures, called *coral polyps*, are similar to sea anemones. They grow joined together in huge colonies. There are thousands of different types of coral. Some look like flowers or tiny trees, others like ferns or sponges. Each coral polyp grows a protective limestone casing. When corals die, the casings are left behind and build up to form a reef, on which new corals grow.

A reef grows incredibly slowly, about half an inch a year, but it can grow to a spectacular size. The Great Barrier Reef, which is the biggest reef of all, stretches for about 1,100 miles (1,770 km) along the northeastern coast of Australia and can be seen from the Moon.

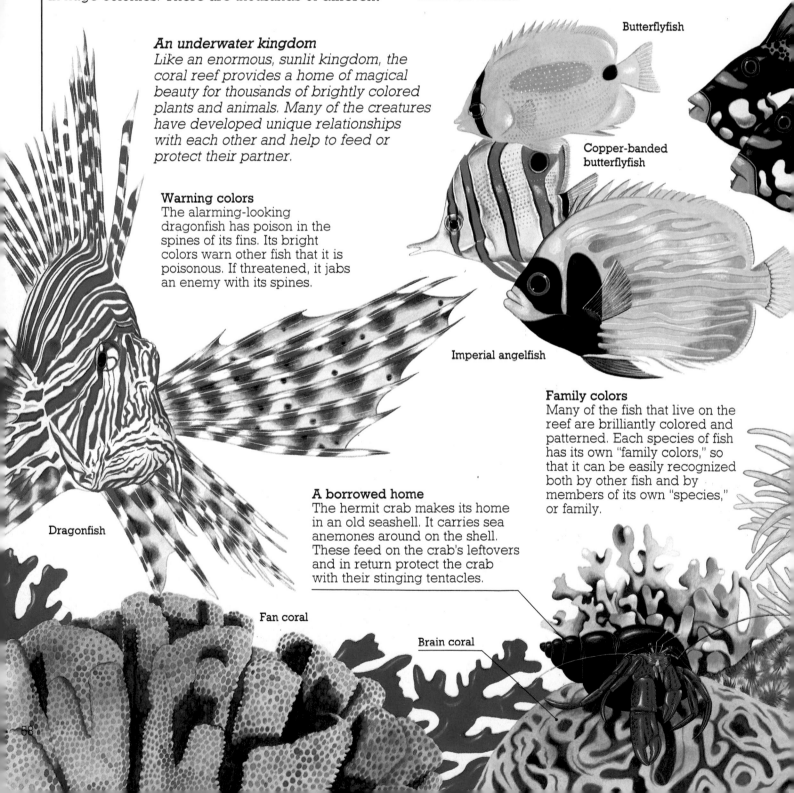

An underwater kingdom
Like an enormous, sunlit kingdom, the coral reef provides a home of magical beauty for thousands of brightly colored plants and animals. Many of the creatures have developed unique relationships with each other and help to feed or protect their partner.

Warning colors
The alarming-looking dragonfish has poison in the spines of its fins. Its bright colors warn other fish that it is poisonous. If threatened, it jabs an enemy with its spines.

Butterflyfish

Copper-banded butterflyfish

Imperial angelfish

Family colors
Many of the fish that live on the reef are brilliantly colored and patterned. Each species of fish has its own "family colors," so that it can be easily recognized both by other fish and by members of its own "species," or family.

A borrowed home
The hermit crab makes its home in an old seashell. It carries sea anemones around on the shell. These feed on the crab's leftovers and in return protect the crab with their stinging tentacles.

Dragonfish

Fan coral

Brain coral

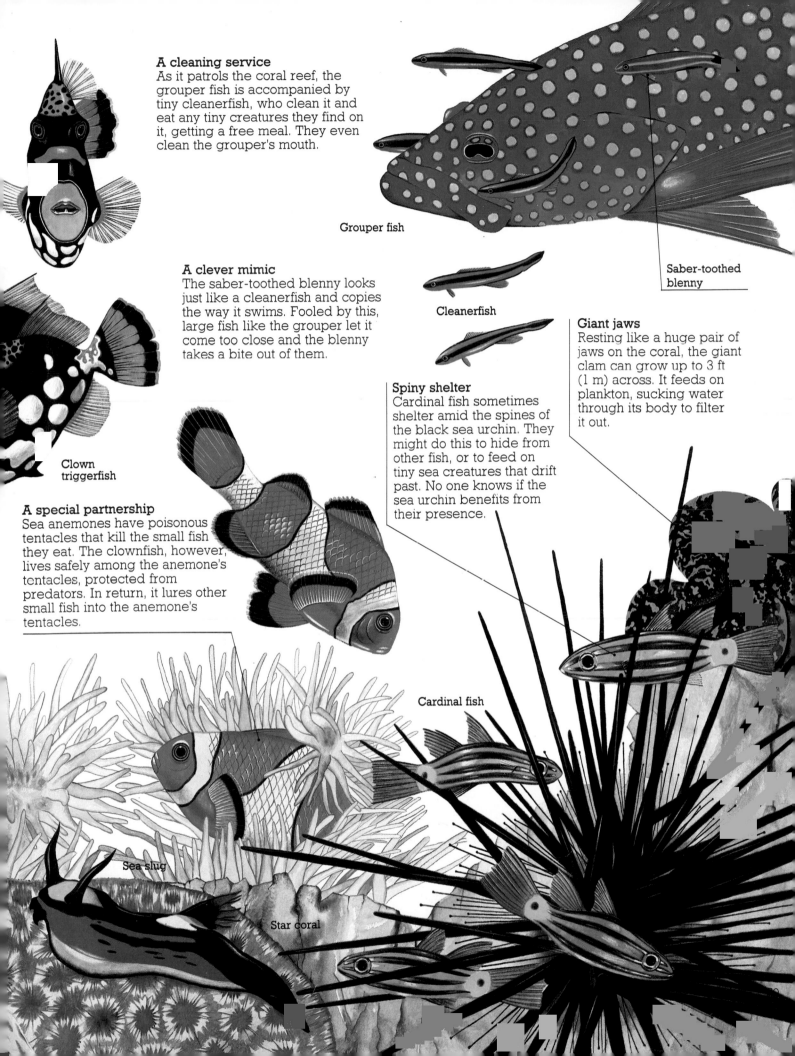

A cleaning service
As it patrols the coral reef, the grouper fish is accompanied by tiny cleanerfish, who clean it and eat any tiny creatures they find on it, getting a free meal. They even clean the grouper's mouth.

Grouper fish

Saber-toothed blenny

A clever mimic
The saber-toothed blenny looks just like a cleanerfish and copies the way it swims. Fooled by this, large fish like the grouper let it come too close and the blenny takes a bite out of them.

Cleanerfish

Giant jaws
Resting like a huge pair of jaws on the coral, the giant clam can grow up to 3 ft (1 m) across. It feeds on plankton, sucking water through its body to filter it out.

Spiny shelter
Cardinal fish sometimes shelter amid the spines of the black sea urchin. They might do this to hide from other fish, or to feed on tiny sea creatures that drift past. No one knows if the sea urchin benefits from their presence.

Clown triggerfish

A special partnership
Sea anemones have poisonous tentacles that kill the small fish they eat. The clownfish, however, lives safely among the anemone's tentacles, protected from predators. In return, it lures other small fish into the anemone's tentacles.

Cardinal fish

Sea slug

Star coral

ANIMALS IN DANGER

Animals are well adapted to natural habitats and for millions of years their numbers have been regulated by the forces of nature. Man has changed all that. By destroying natural habitats, he has endangered the lives of many animals and plants. Unable to adapt to new conditions, many of them have become "extinct" – they have died out completely and no longer exist.

Man has cut down rain forests, used land for farming and built towns, thus destroying many natural habitats. Explorers have opened up areas where animals were once safe from harm, large cats have been killed for their fur and whales hunted to the point of extinction. Lakes, rivers, and the seas have been polluted, and all the time animals are being trapped and sold to wildlife collectors, zoos, and research centers.

Some animals are now officially protected and cannot legally be trapped or killed without permission. Others live in safety in nature preserves or zoos, but unless man stops destroying natural habitats, there will be fewer and fewer places for animals to live, and fewer animals as a result.

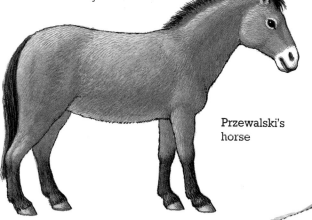

Manatee
The gentle manatee is one of the last survivors of a large family of mammals that lived entirely in water. It is very short-sighted and has been widely hunted for its meat.

Manatee

Quetzal

Quetzal
The quetzal lives in the rain forests of Central America. Prized by the Mayan and Aztec Indians for its tail feathers, it has been hunted by collectors and is now very rare.

Przewalski's horse

California condor

Przewalski's horse
This is the last true wild horse, and used to roam the desolate plains of central China and Mongolia in large herds. It has been saved from extinction by being bred in captivity in zoos.

California condor
Destruction of its habitat, shooting, and pollution have made the California condor nearly extinct. Although the birds have been bred in captivity, it is unknown if the species can be successfully reintroduced to its own habitat.

Extinct animals
Possibly more species of animal have become extinct because of man than have died out naturally before man began to destroy their habitats and kill animals for their skin, fur, or meat. In the rain forests alone, hundreds of species have become extinct in the last two centuries, and thousands more are now at risk.

Dodo

The trusting dodo
Flightless and tame, the dodo was slaughtered for food by sailors on the island of Mauritius. Within 100 years of its discovery it was completely extinct.

Passenger pigeon
Flocks of 2 billion passenger pigeons used to be seen in North America. Through shooting and snaring by man, they were extinct by 1914.

Passenger pigeon

Great auk
Great auks lived in the North Atlantic until about 1852. Clumsy on land, they were battered to death for their fat, meat, and feathers.

Great auk

Blue whale

Blue whale

Blue whale
In the 1930s, there were over 200,000 blue whales, but they were hunted for whale oil and their numbers dropped to fewer than 2,000. Now protected, they number at least 6,000.

Javan rhinoceros
Today, there are fewer than 30 Javan rhinos left in existence, due to hunting and destruction of the rain forest on the overpopulated island of Java. The Javan rhino is now being bred in zoos.

Spanish lynx

Spanish lynx
This lynx used to be widespread in Spain, but much of the forest where it lived has been destroyed. There are now only about 15 pairs left and they live in remote mountainous areas.

Giant panda
There are only about 800-1,000 giant pandas left in the wild, living in remote areas of China. They eat nothing but bamboo, and every 50 years the bamboo dies off mysteriously, causing many pandas to die.

Javan rhinoceros

Gorilla

Gorilla
The largest of the apes, gorillas live in the tropical forests of Central Africa. Their habitat is gradually being destroyed as the forests are cut down and taken over for farming.

Giant panda

Green turtle
Once common in warm, tropical waters, the green turtle has been hunted for its eggs, shell, and meat. A turtle ranch on Bali is reintroducing the species to the wild.

Green turtle

Caspian tiger
The Caspian tiger lived mainly in dense woodland along river valleys in central Russia. Most of these valleys have been destroyed because of land reclamation schemes and this tiger is now on the brink of extinction.

Kiwi

Kiwi
The kiwi is related to the flightless birds called moas that once lived in New Zealand. It has been a protected species since 1896, but is hunted by rats and domestic cats.

Caspian tiger

61

WHAT'S WHAT IN THE ANIMAL WORLD

There are so many different types of animals on Earth – over 10 million *species* or types – that naturalists have divided them up into different groups, to make it easier to work out how they are related to each other. All the members of each group have one or more features in common with each other – a backbone, for example, or a backbone and the same number of legs. Some groups are subdivided into smaller groups, too. Here you can find out about the main groups of animals.

Invertebrates

All animals are classified according to whether or not they have a backbone. Invertebrates are animals without a backbone. Some, like jellyfish, have soft bodies. Others, like insects, have hard, outer skeletons. Insects, arachnids, crustaceans, and mollusks are four different groups of invertebrates.

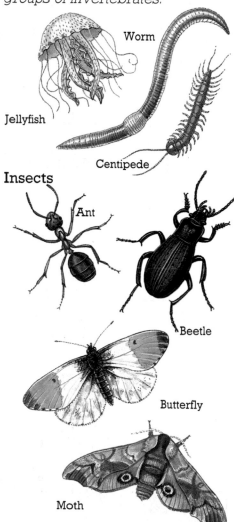

Worm

Jellyfish

Centipede

Insects

Ant

Beetle

Butterfly

Moth

The insects are the largest group of animals on Earth and live everywhere. They have six legs and a body divided into three parts. Most of them have one or two pairs of wings. Ants, beetles, flies, and butterflies are all insects.

Arachnids

Spider

Scorpion

Arachnids have eight legs (two more than insects) and a hard outer skeleton. Their bodies are usually in two parts. Most arachnids are hunters and live on land. They include spiders, scorpions, harvestmen, and mites.

Crustaceans

Woodlice

Shrimp

Crab

Most crustaceans live in water, especially in the sea, like crabs, lobsters, and shrimp. Some, however, like woodlice, live in damp places on land. They all have bodies covered in a hard shell, sometimes in jointed plates.

Mollusks

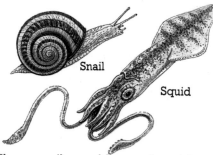

Snail

Squid

Slugs, snails, cockles, and squid are all mollusks. They have soft bodies and sometimes a hard protective shell, but unlike crustaceans, they don't have legs. They mostly live in water and are the second largest group of animals after the insects.

Vertebrates

Vertebrates are animals with backbones and an internal skeleton. There are 46,000 known species of vertebrates. Naturalists have divided them into five main groups: fish, amphibians, reptiles, birds, and mammals. More than half of the different species of vertebrate known are fish.

Fish

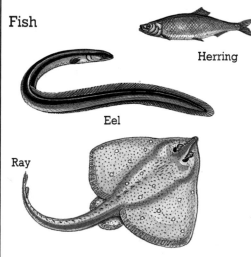

Herring

Eel

Ray

Fish are cold-blooded, which means that their bodies stay the same temperature as their surroundings. They vary a lot in shape, but they nearly all have fins and live in water, breathing through gills. Some live in fresh water, others in the sea.

Amphibians

Frog

Salamander

Amphibians are cold-blooded and have smooth, moist skins without scales or feathers. They can live on land as well as in water, but they have to lay their eggs in damp places. Frogs, toads, salamanders, and newts are all amphibians.

Reptiles

Tortoise

Snake

Crocodile

Reptiles are cold-blooded and have scaly skins. They live on land, as well as in water, and nearly all reptiles lay eggs. Snakes, lizards, tortoises, turtles, and crocodiles are reptiles. Many are carnivorous and eat other animals.

Birds

Duck

Crow

Parrot

Wader

Birds are warm-blooded, which means that their bodies stay the same temperature, regardless of their surroundings. Birds are the only animals with feathers (but their legs are scaly). All of them have wings and most of them can fly.

Mammals

Dolphin

Bat

Cat

The different species of mammal vary enormously, ranging from the dolphin to the bat and the elephant to the dog. They are warm-blooded and the only animals with hair or fur. They feed their newborn babies on milk and have well-developed senses and brains. Rodents, marsupials, and primates are different groups of mammals.

Rodents

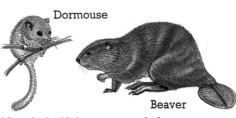

Dormouse

Beaver

Nearly half the mammals known are rodents. Rodent means "gnawing teeth" and all rodents have sharp front teeth. Mice, beavers, chipmunks, and squirrels are rodents. Some of them eat plants and others are scavengers.

Marsupials

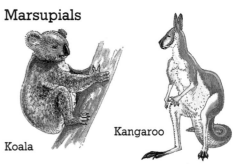

Koala

Kangaroo

Kangaroos, wombats, and koala bears are all marsupials. Many female marsupials have a "pouch" on their undersides. When their babies are born, they are still not fully formed and finish growing inside their mother's warm pouch.

Primates

Bushbaby

Orangutan

Chimpanzee

Lemurs, bushbabies, monkeys, apes, and humans are all primates. Most of them are tree-dwellers and live in tropical rain forests. They look alike, have grasping hands and good eyesight, and are more intelligent than most of the other types of mammals.

63

INDEX

Acknowledgments
Dorling Kindersley would like to thank the following for their help in producing this book: David Bennett, Lynn Bresler, Arthur Brown, Anita Ganeri, Susan Mennell, Denny Robson, and Steve Wooster.